*i*CED *f*OLLIES

iCED fOLLIES

Fantasy cakes for very special occasions

JILL TIPPING

Macdonald Orbis

For Edwin Pouncey, with all my love

A Macdonald Orbis BOOK

© Macdonald & Co (Publishers) Ltd 1988

First published in Great Britain in 1988
by Macdonald & Co (Publishers) Ltd
London & Sydney
A member of Maxwell Pergamon Publishing Corporation plc

British Library Cataloguing in Publication Data
Tipping, Jill
Iced Follies.
1. Cakes. Decoration – Manuals
I. Title
641.8′653

ISBN 0-356-15636-2

Filmset by Tradespools Ltd., Frome.
Printed and bound in Great Britain by
Purnell Book Production Ltd, Paulton

A member of BPCC plc

Senior Commissioning Editor: Joanna Lorenz
Art Director: Bobbie Colegate-Stone
Designer: Sheila Volpe
Illustrator: Sally Kindberg
Photographer: Jerry Tubby
Stylist: Marie O'Hara

Macdonald & Co (Publishers) Ltd
Greater London House
Hampstead Road
London NW1 7QX

CONTENTS

Introduction *6*

BASIC RECIPES, EQUIPMENT & TECHNIQUES

BASIC RECIPES *7*

THE CAKES

iNTRODUCTION

Warning: This book contains cakes which may be considered unsuitable for children. They're not intended for children! Kids have too many cakes designed for them and they can't possibly appreciate your efforts as much as a discerning adult, so let the kids eat bread and use your skills to delight your adult friends with these amazing cakes.

When I make a cake for someone, I try to find out about their interests, hobbies, job, fantasies, habits and memories (usually without them knowing!) and of course the occasion being celebrated. I can then produce something that is very personal, appropriate and a complete surprise. The designs I have dreamt up for this book cover many of these subjects but if none is quite right for you, adapt one to suit. This could mean anything from making the ginger cat in black icing to signify good luck to adjusting the basic shape to make a dog for a dog lover.

Some of the instructions might seem a little daunting but you never know what you can do till you try so get cooking and creating – you may find that you are the one most surprised by your artistic abilities.

BASIC RECIPES, EQUIPMENT AND TECHNIQUES

The art of making fantasy cakes is reliant not only on artistic decorating techniques but also on successful baking to achieve moist, tasty and firm cakes that are easy to cut and shape. Basic recipes for sponge and fruit cakes follow, and methods for making icing and fillings. There is an equipment checklist and technique section showing you the best way to prepare and decorate your cakes with useful step-by-step instructions.

Basic Recipes

RICH FRUIT CAKE

A rich fruit cake is ideal for making more complicated fantasy cakes. The texture is firm, and the cake will remain moist and full of flavour once it has been covered in marzipan and icing. It is firm enough to cut into intricate shapes, to support other pieces of cake and, when iced, produces a smooth even finish. This cake will cut into small neat pieces and, because of the richness, will serve many more people. For example, a 20 cm (8 inch) square cake can yield 40–50 portions.

Line the base and sides of the tin with a double thickness of greaseproof paper (see pages 20–21 on lining tins). Secure a double-thickness strip of brown wrapping paper around the outside of the tin with string. Stand the cake tin on a couple of sheets of brown paper or newspaper in the oven. To prevent the top of the cake becoming over-browned, cover the top with a double thickness of greaseproof paper for the last third of cooking time.

Leave the cake to cool in the tin, then turn out and remove the lining paper. Re-wrap in clean greaseproof paper or foil, then place in an airtight tin where it will keep for months. This cake improves with keeping but is delicious if eaten immediately. For extra flavour and moisture, pierce holes into the top of the cake with a skewer and pour in extra brandy or rum.

The Rich Fruit Cake recipe chart on page 10 produces cakes measuring 7.5 cm (3 inches) in depth. To calculate the quantity of cake mixture needed for recipes using odd-shaped tins or bowls, follow this method.

1 Fill the chosen shaped tin or bowl with water to the depth of the cake required.

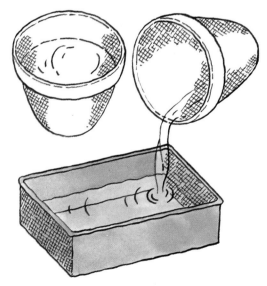

2 Pour into a regular tin to the same water level – try various tins to find the correct size.
3 Follow the recipe for the given quantity on the chart to match this tin size and shape.

Basic Method for Rich Fruit Cake

See chart on page 10.

1 Preheat the oven to 140°C (275°F/Gas Mark 1). Grease and double line the required cake tin (see instructions on page 20).

2 Place the glacé cherries, almonds, mixed peel, dried fruit, lemon zest and brandy or rum in a large mixing bowl. Mix well together.

3 Place the butter or margarine and sugar in a mixing bowl. Mix together with a wooden spoon, then beat until light and fluffy.

4 Add the eggs a little at a time, beating well after each addition, until all the egg has been incorporated and the mixture is soft and glossy. If it looks slightly curdled, beat in 1–2 tablespoons of the flour.

5 Sift the flour and mixed spice into the bowl. Using a spatula or a large spoon, carefully fold in the flour, cutting through and turning the mixture until all the flour has been incorporated.

6 Add the cake mixture to the mixed fruit in the bowl and mix together until all the fruit has been evenly distributed.

7 Place the cake mixture in the prepared tin. Smooth the surface and make a slight depression in the centre to ensure a level top when the cake has cooked.

8 Bake the cake in the centre of the oven for the recommended cooking time (see chart). Test the cake 15 minutes before the recommended cooking time is up, then at regular intervals until the cake is cooked. (A skewer inserted for 5 seconds should come out clean.) Cool in the tin.

LIGHT FRUIT CAKE

This moist fruit cake is a delicious alternative to a rich fruit cake for those who prefer a lighter cake. As there is less fruit in the mixture, the keeping qualities are not as good as a rich fruit cake. However, wrapped in cling film and kept in a tin, or marzipanned and iced, this cake will keep for several months.

If preferred, the mixture of fruit may be varied to include mixed glacé fruits and nuts, such as glacé plums, pineapple, apricots, brazils or walnuts. This will give the cake a colourful appearance when cut into slices.

Fill odd-shaped tins and bowls as described in the Rich Fruit Cake introduction on page 7, adjusting the cooking times as necessary.

Basic Method for Light Fruit Cake

See chart on page 11.

1 Preheat the oven to 170°C (325°F/Gas Mark 3). Grease and line the required cake tin (see instructions on page 20).

2 Place the dried fruit, glacé cherries, mixed peel, orange zest and juice and rum in a large mixing bowl. Mix well together.

3 Place the butter or margarine and sugar in a mixing bowl. Mix together with a wooden spoon, then beat until light and fluffy.

4 Add the eggs a little at a time, beating well after each addition, until all the egg has been incorporated and the mixture is soft and glossy. If it looks slightly curdled, beat in 1–2 tablespoons of the flour. Stir in ground almonds.

5 Sift the flour into the bowl. Using a spatula or a large spoon, carefully fold in the flour, cutting through and turning the mixture until all the flour has been incorporated.

6 Add the cake mixture to the mixed fruit in the bowl and mix together until all the fruit has been evenly distributed.

7 Place the cake mixture in the prepared tin. Smooth the surface and make a slight depression in the centre to ensure a level top.

8 Bake the cake in the centre of the oven for the recommended cooking time (see chart). Test the cake (a skewer inserted for 5 seconds should come out clean) at regular intervals until the cake is cooked. Cool in the tin.

QUICK SPONGE CAKE

This cake mixture is ideal for many of the fantasy cakes in this book. It has a very light texture but can be easily cut into different shapes. See chart for flavour variations.

Make the sponge at least a day before using it, allowing the cake to settle and making it easier to handle. It is very simple to make as all the ingredients are just mixed together, then baked. Sponge cakes will keep for 2–3 days wrapped in cling film or kept in a tin, or if preferred double wrap and freeze until required.

Always use ingredients at room temperature, except soft margarine which may be used straight from the refrigerator. Do not add more baking powder than stated in the recipe and do not overbeat the mixture as this will cause the cake to over-rise, then sink in the centre.

The quantity of cake mixture needed for recipes using odd-shaped tins or bowls may be calculated as described in the Rich Fruit Cake introduction on page 7. Remember that a deep cake mixture will take longer to cook than a shallow cake mixture using the same size tin, so the chart baking times will vary.

Basic Method for Quick Sponge Cake

See chart on page 12.

1 Preheat the oven to 170°C (325°F/Gas Mark 3). Grease and line the required cake tin (see instructions on page 20).

2 Place all the ingredients in a large mixing bowl. Mix together with a wooden spoon, then beat until smooth and glossy.

3 Put the mixture into the prepared tin and smooth the surface. Bake the cake in the centre of the oven for the recommended cooking time (see chart). Test the cake by pressing the centre with the fingers; the cake should feel firm and springy when cooked.

4 Loosen the edges with a palette knife if the tin is not paper lined, and invert onto a cooling rack. Remove the lining paper and turn the cake the right way up to cool.

VICTORIA SPONGE CAKE

This is the traditional way of making a sponge cake, by creaming together the butter or margarine and sugar to incorporate the air before gradually adding the remaining ingredients. This produces a very similar sponge to the Quick Sponge Cake, but with a lighter texture.

Different flavourings may be added to the cake mixture to give variety. Try adding orange zest for a delicious orange-flavoured cake, or a mixture of blended coffee and cocoa for a mocha cake. See chart for flavour variations.

The quantity of cake mixture needed for recipes using odd-shaped tins or bowls may be calculated as described in the Rich Fruit Cake introduction on page 7.

Remember that a deep cake mixture will take longer to cook than a shallow mixture using the same size tin, so the chart baking times will vary.

Basic Method for Victoria Sponge Cake

See chart on page 13.

1 Preheat the oven to 170°C (325°F/Gas Mark 3). Grease and line the required cake tin (see instructions on page 20).

2 Place the butter or margarine and sugar in a mixing bowl. Mix together with a wooden spoon, then beat until light and fluffy.

3 Add the eggs a little at a time, beating well after each addition, until all the egg has been incorporated and the mixture is soft and glossy. If it looks slightly curdled, beat in 1–2 tablespoons of the flour.

4 Sift the flour into the bowl and add any flavourings if required. Using a spatula or a large spoon, carefully fold in the flour, cutting through and turning the mixture until all the flour has been incorporated.

5 Put the mixture into the prepared tin and smooth the surface. Bake the cake in the centre of the oven for the recommended cooking time (see chart). Test the cake by pressing the centre with the fingers; the cake should feel firm and springy when cooked.

6 Loosen the edges with a palette knife if the tin is not paper lined, and invert onto a cooling rack. Remove the lining paper and turn the cake the right way up to cool.

RICH FRUIT CAKE CHART

The quantities given below are for 7.5 cm (3 inch) deep cake tins. Cooking times are approximate as individual ovens do vary.

CAKE TIN SIZES	Square: Round:	12 cm (5 in) 15 cm (6 in)	15 cm (6 in) 18 cm (7 in)	18 cm (7 in) 20 cm (8 in)	20 cm (8 in) 23 cm (9 in)	23 cm (9 in) 25 cm (10 in)	25 cm (10 in) 28 cm (11 in)
Glacé cherries, quartered		50 g (2 oz)	75 g (3 oz)	150 g (5½ oz)	175 g (6 oz)	250 g (9 oz)	275 g (10 oz)
Almonds, blanched and chopped		25 g (1 oz)	50 g (2 oz)	75 g (3 oz)	125 g (4½ oz)	150 g (5½ oz)	200 g (7 oz)
Mixed peel		25 g (1 oz)	50 g (2 oz)	75 g (3 oz)	125 g (4½ oz)	150 g (5½ oz)	200 g (7 oz)
Mixed dried fruit		425 g (15 oz)	650 g (1 lb 7 oz)	850 g (1 lb 14 oz)	1.075 kg (2 lb 6 oz)	1.5 kg (3 lb 5 oz)	1.875 kg (4 lb 2 oz)
Lemon zest, finely grated		5 ml (1 tsp)	7.5 ml (1½ tsp)	10 ml (2 tsp)	12.5 ml (2½ tsp)	15 ml (3 tsp)	17.5 ml (3½ tsp)
Brandy or rum		15 ml (1 tbsp)	15 ml (1 tbsp)	22.5 ml (1½ tbsp)	30 ml (2 tbsp)	37.5 ml (2½ tbsp)	45 ml (3 tbsp)
Butter or margarine, softened		150 g (5½ oz)	175 g (6 oz)	275 g (10 oz)	350 g (12 oz)	500 g (1 lb 2 oz)	600 g (1 lb 5 oz)
Soft dark brown sugar		150 g (5½ oz)	175 g (6 oz)	275 g (10 oz)	350 g (12 oz)	500 g (1 lb 2 oz)	600 g (1 lb 5 oz)
Eggs (size 3)		2	3	5	6	8	9
Plain flour		200 g (7 oz)	225 g (8 oz)	350 g (12 oz)	400 g (14 oz)	600 g (1 lb 5 oz)	675 g (1 lb 8 oz)
Ground mixed spice		2.5 ml (½ tsp)	5 ml (1 tsp)	7.5 ml (1½ tsp)	10 ml (2 tsp)	12.5 ml (2½ tsp)	15 ml (3 tsp)
Oven temperature		140°C (275°F/ Gas Mark 1)	140°C (275°F/ Gas Mark 1)	140°C (275°F/ Gas Mark 1)	140°C (275°F/ Gas Mark 1)	140° (275°F/ Gas Mark 1)	140°C (275°F/ Gas Mark 1)
Approximate cooking time		3¼ hours	3¾ hours	4¾ hours	5½ hours	6½ hours	7¾ hours

LIGHT FRUIT CAKE CHART

*The quantities given below are for 7.5 cm (3 inch)
deep cake tins. Cooking times are approximate as
individual ovens do vary.*

CAKE TIN SIZES	Square: Round:	12 cm (5 in) 15 cm (6 in)	15 cm (6 in) 18 cm (7 in)	18 cm (7 in) 20 cm (8 in)	20 cm (8 in) 23 cm (9 in)	23 cm (9 in) 25 cm (10 in)	25 cm (10 in) 28 cm (11 in)
Mixed dried fruit		150 g (5½ oz)	175 g (6 oz)	275 g (10 oz)	350 g (12 oz)	550 g (1 lb 3 oz)	600 g (1 lb 5 oz)
Glacé cherries, quartered		50 g (2 oz)	125 g (4½ oz)	175 g (6 oz)	225 g (8 oz)	275 g (10 oz)	350 g (12 oz)
Mixed peel		25 g (1 oz)	50 g (2 oz)	75 g (3 oz)	125 g (4½ oz)	150 g (5½ oz)	200 g (7 oz)
Orange zest, finely grated		2.5 ml (½ tsp)	5 ml (1 tsp)	7.5 ml (1½ tsp)	10 ml (2 tsp)	12.5 ml (2½ tsp)	15 ml (3 tsp)
Orange juice		15 ml (1 tbsp)	15 ml (1 tbsp)	30 ml (2 tbsp)	30 ml (2 tbsp)	45 ml (3 tbsp)	60 ml (4 tbsp)
Rum		15 ml (1 tbsp)	30 ml (2 tbsp)	30 ml (2 tbsp)	45 ml (3 tbsp)	45 ml (3 tbsp)	60 ml (4 tbsp)
Butter or margarine, softened		75 g (3 oz)	125 g (4½ oz)	200 g (7 oz)	225 g (8 oz)	325 g (11½ oz)	350 g (12 oz)
Caster sugar		75 g (3 oz)	125 g (4½ oz)	200 g (7 oz)	225 g (8 oz)	325 g (11½ oz)	350 g (12 oz)
Eggs (size 3)		1	2	3	4	5	6
Ground almonds		15 g (½ oz)	25 g (1 oz)	40 g (1½ oz)	50 g (2 oz)	75 g (3 oz)	100 g (4 oz)
Self-raising flour		125 g (4½ oz)	150 g (5½ oz)	225 g (8 oz)	250 g (9 oz)	350 g (12 oz)	400 g (14 oz)
Oven temperature		170°C (325°F/ Gas Mark 3)	170°C (325°F/ Gas Mark 3)	170°C (325°F/ Gas Mark 3)	170°C (325°F/ Gas Mark 3)	170° (325°F/ Gas Mark 3)	170°C (325°F/ Gas Mark 3)
Approximate cooking time		1½ hours	2 hours	2½ hours	3 hours	3½ hours	4 hours

QUICK SPONGE CAKE CHART

*The quantities given below are for 7.5 cm (3 inch)
deep cake tins. Cooking times are approximate as
individual ovens do vary.*

CAKE TIN SIZES		12 cm (5 in) 15 cm (6 in)	15 cm (6 in) 18 cm (7 in)	18 cm (7 in) 20 cm (8 in)	20 cm (8 in) 23 cm (9 in)	23 cm (9 in) 25 cm (10 in)	25 cm (10 in) 28 cm (11 in)	28 cm (11 in) 30 cm (12 in)
	Square: *Round:*							
Self-raising flour		175 g (6 oz)	225 g (8 oz)	275 g (10 oz)	350 g (12 oz)	400 g (14 oz)	450 g (1 lb)	500 g (1 lb 2 oz)
Baking powder		2.5 ml (½ tsp)	5 ml (1 tsp)	5 ml (1 tsp)	5 ml (1 tsp)	10 ml (2 tsp)	10 ml (2 tsp)	10 ml (2 tsp)
Caster sugar		100 g (4 oz)	175 g (6 oz)	225 g (8 oz)	275 g (10 oz)	350 g (12 oz)	400 g (14 oz)	450 g (1 lb)
Butter or margarine softened		100 g (4 oz)	175 g (6 oz)	225 g (8 oz)	275 g (10 oz)	350 g (12 oz)	400 g (14 oz)	450 g (1 lb)
Eggs (size 3)		2	3	4	5	6	7	8
Milk or citrus juice		10 ml (2 tsp)	15 ml (1 tbsp)	30 ml (2 tbsp)	45 ml (3 tbsp)	53 ml (3½ tbsp)	60 ml (4 tbsp)	68 ml (4½ tbsp)
VARIATIONS *Chocolate:* cocoa replaces same of the flour		15 g (½ oz)	25 g (1 oz)	40 g (1½ oz)	40 g (1½ oz)	50 g (2 oz)	50 g (2 oz)	65 g (2½ oz)
Peppermint: add essence or oil		2.5 ml (½ tsp)	5 ml (1 tsp)	7.5 ml (1½ tsp)	7.5 ml (1½ tsp)	10 ml (2 tsp)	10 ml (2 tsp)	12.5 ml (2½ tsp)
Citrus: add orange, lemon or lime zest, finely grated		5 ml (1 tsp)	7.5 ml (1½ tsp)	10 ml (2 tsp)	12½ ml (2½ tsp)	15 ml (3 tsp)	17.5 ml (3½ tsp)	20 ml (4 tsp)
Oven temperature		170°C (325°F/ Gas Mark 3)	170°C (325°F/ Gas Mark 3)	170°C (325°F/ Gas Mark 3)	170°C (325°F/ Gas Mark 3)	170° (325°F/ Gas Mark 3)	170°C (325°F/ Gas Mark 3)	170°C (325°F/ Gas Mark 3)
Approximate cooking time		50 minutes	1 hour	1¼ hours	1½ hours	1¾ hours	1¾ hours	2 hours

VICTORIA SPONGE CAKE CHART

The quantities given below are for 7.5 cm (3 inch) deep cake tins. Cooking times are approximate as individual ovens do vary.

CAKE TIN SIZES	*Square:* *Round:*	12 cm (5 in) 15 cm (6 in)	15 cm (6 in) 18 cm (7 in)	18 cm (7 in) 20 cm (8 in)	20 cm (8 in) 23 cm (9 in)	23 cm (9 in) 25 cm (10 in)	25 cm (10 in) 28 cm (11 in)	28 cm (11 in) 30 cm (12 in)
Butter or margarine, softened		50 g (2 oz)	125 g (4½ oz)	175 g (6 oz)	225 g (8 oz)	350 g (12 oz)	450 g (1 lb)	500 g (1 lb 2 oz)
Caster sugar		50 g (2 oz)	125 g (4½ oz)	175 g (6 oz)	225 g (8 oz)	350 g (12 oz)	450 g (1 lb)	500 g (1 lb 2 oz)
Eggs (size 3)		1	2	3	4	6	8	9
Self-raising flour		50 g (2 oz)	125 g (4½ oz)	175 g (6 oz)	225 g (8 oz)	350 g (12 oz)	450 g (1 lb)	500 g (1 lb 2 oz)
VARIATIONS *Chocolate:* substitute cocoa for same of the flour		15 ml (1 tbsp)	22.5 ml (1½ tbsp)	25 g (1 oz)	35 g (1¼ oz)	45 g (1¾ oz)	50 g (2 oz)	65 g (2½ oz)
Citrus: add orange, lemon or lime zest, finely grated		5 ml (1 tsp)	10 ml (2 tsp)	15 ml (1 tbsp)	22.5 ml (1½ tbsp)	30 ml (2 tbsp)	37.5 ml (2½ tbsp)	37.5 ml (2½ tbsp)
Cherry and almond: add 1. glacé cherries, chopped		25 g (1 oz)	50 g (2 oz)	100 g (4 oz)	125 g (4½ oz)	150 g (5½ oz)	175 g (6 oz)	225 g (8 oz)
2. Almond essence		2.5 ml (½ tsp)	5 ml (1 tsp)	7.5 ml (1½ tsp)	10 ml (2 tsp)	12.5 ml (2½ tsp)	15 ml (3 tsp)	17.5 ml (3½ tsp)
Oven temperature		170°C (325°F/ Gas Mark 3)	170°C (325°F/ Gas Mark 3)	170°C (325°F/ Gas Mark 3)	170°C (325°F/ Gas Mark 3)	170° (325°F/ Gas Mark 3)	170°C (325°F/ Gas Mark 3)	170°C (325°F/ Gas Mark 3)
Approximate cooking time		30 minutes	40 minutes	50 minutes	1 hour	1¼ hours	1½ hours	1¾ hours

SWISS ROLL

Although it is easier to buy a ready-made Swiss roll from the supermarket, you may like to know how to make your own. This light, fat-free sponge is suitable for making large slabs of sponge cake, ideal for cutting into unusual shapes for fantasy cakes as well as for Swiss rolls.

Cakes made from this recipe are delicious when first made, and keep moist and fresh once they have been completely iced; otherwise they have a tendency to go dry.

Basic Swiss Roll Quantity and Method

3 eggs (size 3)
100 g (4 oz) caster sugar
100 g (4 oz) plain flour, sifted
pinch of salt
caster sugar to sprinkle
60 ml (4 tbsp) jam, warmed

1 Preheat the oven to 180°C (350°F/Gas Mark 4). Grease and line the base of a 33 × 23 cm (13 × 9 inch) Swiss roll tin.

2 Place the eggs and sugar in a heatproof bowl over a saucepan of hot but not boiling water. Whisk the mixture until thick and pale. Remove the bowl from the saucepan and continue whisking until, when the whisk is lifted, it leaves a trail of mixture on the surface.

3 Sift the flour and salt onto the surface of the mixture. Using a spatula or a large spoon, carefully fold in the flour, cutting through and turning the mixture until all the flour has been incorporated.

4 Pour the mixture into the prepared tin and gently level the top with a spatula. Bake in the centre of the oven for 10–15 minutes. Test the cake by pressing the centre with the fingers; the cake should feel firm and springy when cooked.

5 To make a Swiss roll from the sponge, cut out a piece of non-stick baking parchment or greaseproof paper 2.5 cm (1 inch) larger than the tin and sprinkle with caster sugar.

6 Invert the cooked cake onto the sugared paper with the short end towards you; carefully remove the lining paper.

7 Trim a 5 mm (¼ inch) off each side of the cake and spread the surface evenly with warm jam. Fold the far short edge over by 1 cm (½ inch), then roll up with the aid of the paper, pulling the roll towards you.

8 Leave to set in the paper for 5 minutes on a cooling rack, then carefully remove and leave the Swiss roll with the join underneath until completely cold.

ROYAL ICING

Royal icing makes a harder covering for cakes and, since it can be sanded down between coats, can make sharp square corners and flat surfaces for a more formal cake. It is also used to fix decorations to a cake and, most of all in this book, for delicate piping techniques. You can buy packets of instant royal icing, which are just mixed with water, for small quantities of icing.

This recipe will make 225 g (8 oz) royal icing of a consistency that dries hard enough for piping but which can be cut easily if applied to a cake in thin layers. To make larger amounts of icing, increase the ingredients proportionally. Egg albumen powder can also be used instead of egg white to save having leftover egg yolks. Placing a cake in a moist atmosphere (like a steamy kitchen) will also make it easier to cut, or add 2–3 drops of glycerine to the mixture for a softer icing, but do not use this for piping or run-outs which need to dry hard. A little acetic acid, cream of tartar or gum tragacanth added to the mixture will make harder icing for pieces to be used in a structure.

Basic Quantity and Method

1 small egg white
225 g (8 oz) icing sugar
5 ml (1 tsp) lemon juice

1 Beat the egg white until frothy in a mixing bowl. Sift the icing sugar and slowly add to the mixture, beating well. Stir the lemon juice into the mixture.

2 Place a damp tea towel on top of the icing or put in an airtight container to prevent it from drying out.

FONDANT ICING

Fondant icing, also known as sugar paste, modelling fondant or moulding icing, is used on most of the cakes in this book. It can be bought from supermarkets in small packets and from specialist cake decorating shops (see page 166 for a list) in 450 g (1 lb) slabs or in bulk. It is soft and pliable and can be rolled out like marzipan to cover cakes. It can be moulded like clay to make decorations yet dries hard enough for making self-supporting objects; it can easily be painted and still remains soft enough to cut. Colour can be kneaded into the icing easily (see page 23).

Bought fondant icing will keep for weeks if tightly wrapped in a plastic bag, but here is a recipe to make 450 g (1 lb) fondant – to make more increase the ingredients proportionally. To make 675 g (1½ lb) fondant you will need 75 g (3 oz) liquid glucose, 2 small egg whites and 675 g (1½ lb) icing; to make 900 g (2 lb) fondant you will need 100 g (4 oz) liquid glucose, 2 large egg whites and 900 g (2 lb) icing sugar.

Remember to remove any rings before putting your hands into the mixture as it is a very sticky mixture to work with. Keep wrapped in aluminium foil or cling film – it will remain soft for about 24 hours kept this way. Roll out and mould fondant using a little icing sugar for dusting to help prevent any sticking. Cornflour can also be used, but it can make the icing dry.

Basic Quantity and Method

50 g (2 oz) liquid glucose
1 large egg white
450 g (1 lb) icing sugar
icing sugar or cornflour for dusting

1 Blend the glucose and egg white together in a large mixing bowl. (Stand the glucose jar in hot water to soften if necessary.) Sift the icing sugar and add in small amounts, beating well, until the mixture resembles a smooth paste.

2 When the mixture is very stiff, turn out onto a surface dusted with icing sugar or cornflour. Knead until smooth and firm. Add a little water to the fondant if it feels dry.

3 Keep the fondant in cling film or aluminium foil until needed and colour as required.

MARZIPAN

Almond paste or marzipan is used to cover fruit cakes to help prevent the icing from being discoloured by the cake and also to provide a smooth surface for decoration. White marzipan can be coloured and moulded into decorations such as small animals or fruit and can also be painted directly with food colours.

White marzipan is now available from most supermarkets. It is very pliable, can be easily moulded and coloured, is tasty, and above all, convenient to use. Quality marzipan with a higher almond content is available from specialist cake decorating shops (see page 166 for a list) but if you want to make your own, here is a simple recipe that requires no cooking.

Marzipan can be kept for up to two years if well wrapped in aluminium foil or cling film and kept in a cool place. This basic quantity makes 450 g (1 lb) of marzipan, which is sufficient to cover a 18 cm (7 inch) or 20 cm (8 inch) round fruit cake. To make more marzipan, increase all the ingredients proportionally.

Basic Quantity and Method

225 g (8 oz) ground almonds
100 g (4 oz) caster sugar
100 g (4 oz) icing sugar
2 small eggs
2.5 ml (½ tsp) lemon juice
almond essence

1 Put the almonds and the sugars in a mixing bowl and blend together.

2 Beat the eggs well with the lemon juice and a few drops of almond essence, than add to the almond mixture. Mix to a workable paste, with your hands, if necessary.

3 Wrap the marzipan in aluminium foil or cling film to keep it from drying out and store in a cool place until needed.

GLACÉ ICING

This quick icing for cakes is particularly useful in fantasy cake making where you need something that looks liquid, like paint or drinks. Use quickly once mixed as it soon crusts and starts to dry. This basic quantity makes 175 g (6 oz) icing, which is sufficient to cover an 18 cm (7 inch) round cake. To make larger amounts of glacé icing increase the ingredients proportionally.

Basic Quantity and Method

175 g (6 oz) icing sugar

30 ml (2 tbsp) warm water

1 Sift the icing sugar into a mixing bowl and gradually add the warm water until the icing is thick enough to coat the back of a spoon. Add more water or sugar to change the consistency. To make icing of a finer texture, heat the ingredients in a small saucepan until warm. The icing should look smooth and glossy.

VARIATIONS

Orange or Lemon Icing: substitute 30 ml (2 tbsp) orange or lemon juice for the water.

Chocolate Icing: dissolve 30 ml (2 tbsp) cocoa in a little warm water and add to the mixture.

Coffee Icing: mix 5 ml (1 tsp) coffee essence into the prepared icing.

CHEWY CHOCOLATE COVERING

This pliable chocolate icing is good for moulding small decorations as well as covering cakes. It is most successful when made with plain chocolate, but can be made with milk or white chocolate. A less expensive version could be made with chocolate flavour cake covering. If liked, a little paste food colouring can be added to give soft colours.

This covering will stay reasonably soft if kept at room temperature, so if decorations do wilt a little, 10 minutes in the refrigerator will be sufficient to harden them. Roll out the covering on an icing sugar dusted board or, for a really clean finish, between sheets of non-stick baking paper. Cut up with a sharp knife or scissors.

This basic quantity will make 100 g (4 oz) chewy chocolate. Increase the ingredients listed below proportionally to make larger amounts of the covering.

Basic Quantity and Method

100 g (4 oz) chocolate

30 ml (2 tbsp) liquid glucose

food colouring (optional)

1 Stand the jar of liquid glucose in a bowl of hot water to soften it.

2 Melt the chocolate in a saucepan over a gentle heat. Alternatively, melt in the microwave on full power for 1–2 minutes.

3 Remove from the heat or microwave and stir in the glucose (food colouring can also be added at this point). Pour into a large china or Pyrex bowl and leave to cool completely.

4 Knead the ingredients together in the bowl with your hands until smooth, then roll out on an icing sugar dusted board or between sheets of non-stick paper as required.

BUTTERCREAM

Sweet and creamy in texture, this is a traditional topping and filling for sponge cakes. Although it is easily varied in flavour, buttercream does not take colour very well, so aim to use pale shades using liquid food colours to tint it and bear in mind that its basic creamy tone will affect the colour, making blue slightly greenish and pink or violet, peachy or brown. It can be piped in simple designs but will become runny in warm hands so you will need to work quickly.

When soft and low fat margarines are used, omit the milk or water. The basic quantity makes 350 g (12 oz) buttercream which will completely cover and fill an 18 cm (7 inch) round cake. Increase or decrease the ingredients proportionally for larger or smaller amounts of buttercream.

Basic Quantity and Method

100 g (4 oz) butter, cut into small pieces
225 g (8 oz) icing sugar, sifted
few drops vanilla essence
15–30 ml (1–2 tbsp) milk or warm water

1 Cream the butter until soft in a mixing bowl. An electric mixer can be used, if preferred.

2 Slowly add the icing sugar, vanilla and the milk or water, and beat until the mixture is light and fluffy in texture.

VARIATIONS

Orange or lemon buttercream: leave out the vanilla essence and add some grated orange or lemon zest and some juice; beat well to prevent curdling.

Walnut or almond buttercream: mix in 30 ml (2 tbsp) finely chopped walnuts or almonds to the buttercream.

Coffee buttercream: leave out the vanilla essence and add 10 ml (2 tsp) coffee powder mixed with water or 15 ml (1 tbsp) coffee essence to the buttercream.

Chocolate buttercream: add 25–40 g (1–1½ oz) of melted chocolate to the buttercream or 15 ml (1 tbsp) cocoa powder dissolved in some hot water; cool before adding to the mixture.

Hazelnut chocolate buttercream: add 100 g (4 oz) chocolate hazelnut spread to the chocolate buttercream mixture. This will make 450 g (1 lb) buttercream.

APRICOT GLAZE

Apricot jam can be spread straight from the jar with a knife (avoiding the pieces of fruit) onto plain square and round cakes to attach marzipan. Make apricot glaze for brushing with a pastry brush onto more complex shaped fruit cakes, onto sponge cakes to keep down the crumbs, and to attach fondant icing.

Cheap apricot jam tends to have the least whole fruit in it, making it easier to sieve.

Basic Quantity and Method

450 g (1 lb) apricot jam
15 ml (1 tbsp) lemon juice
60 ml (4 tbsp) water

1 Sieve the jam into a small saucepan. Add the juice and water and cook, stirring over a low heat until the jam has completely melted.

2 Brush the glaze while still hot over a fruit cake, but allow to cool slightly before spreading over a sponge cake. Store the remaining glaze in a screw-top jar and use as required.

Equipment

There is little essential equipment needed for making cakes. Apart from the obvious cooking utensils and bowls and of course cake tins (which can be hired at many specialist shops, see p. 166), all you really need to get started is a good rolling pin and a sharp pointed knife. You will find that you can use many things you have around the kitchen and the home for decorating purposes until you feel serious enough to spend money on special equipment. Make sure all the equipment you use is clean, dry and also non-toxic – avoid using painted items.

ARTIST'S PAINT BRUSHES

A quality fine-pointed artist's paint brush is invaluable for painting faces and other small details onto fantasy cakes. Sable brushes are expensive but do give the best line and will last well if treated with respect.

Do not leave a brush standing in a jar of water as this will permanently bend the hairs. Wash it thoroughly when changing colours and after use with a little washing up liquid in the palm of your hand, then rinse well.

CAKE BOARDS AND DRUMS

These are both available in many different sizes, even hexagons and hearts, in silver and gold, from department stores and kitchen shops. Throughout this book a thin board (up to 3 mm/1/8 inch thick) is referred to as a board and a thick one (about 1 cm/1/2 inch thick) as a drum. But the boards specified in the book are not always available in shops – some have been cut from larger boards while others are pieces of thick cardboard, hardboard or chipboard cut to the right size – see page 20 for covering boards.

CAKE TINS

There is a wide variety of cake tins available – different sizes of squares, circles and rectangles as well as hexagons, ovals, hearts and numbers. Ovenproof pudding basins and bowls and empty food cans can all be used to achieve different cake shapes. See page 7 for assessing the amount of cake mixture required when using odd-shaped tins.

COCKTAIL STICKS/SKEWERS

Because they are made to use with food, wooden cocktail sticks and skewers are invaluable for joining cakes together and supporting icing details without affecting the flavour.

Cocktail sticks are also good for taking liquid food colours from bottles (drinking straws are also ideal for this) and paste colours from tubs to add to icing. Use one stick for each colour and you will keep the colours in the tubs clean.

CUTTERS

Cups, glasses, jar tops, spice tubs and lids, piping tubes, pen tops and straws provide an extensive range of circular cutters readily found in the cook's kitchen. The sharpest edge to the cut-outs is obtained from thin plastic and glass but edges can always be tidied up with a knife.

More complex shapes can be cut around home-made cardboard templates but it is best for consistency of shape to use proper cutters for large numbers of stars, hearts, petals or leaves. Made from stainless steel, cutters are available in a huge range of sizes and shapes from large biscuit to small aspic shapes; from plain circles to different types of flowers.

ICING SMOOTHERS

You can use a rolling pin to flatten the top of a marzipan- or fondant-covered cake, and a straight-sided glass bottle or tumbler to smooth the sides. Plastic smoothers with handles are also available to do this – they are particularly good for producing sharp corners on a square cake but not essential.

A flat scraper is best for obtaining a smooth finish on royal icing and you can get serrated ones to create special effects.

KNIVES

Knives should be sharp, not serrated and – especially for cutting fondant icing – the blade should be as thin and flat as possible. A large cook's knife will cut a straight line in marzipan or fondant without having to drag it along, and a small pointed craft knife is good for cutting out small pieces and modelling details.

MIXING BOWLS

Glass and china bowls are the best types to use to avoid discoloration of icing. They should be absolutely grease-free when mixing royal icing. Dessert or soup bowls and cups are useful for mixing food colouring into small quantities of royal icing.

MODELLING TOOLS

Knives, round and flat skewers, knitting needles, bodkins and other small handy items were used for modelling marzipan and fondant throughout the cake recipes in this book. It is also possible to buy a set of professional modelling tools in a range of shapes, including shell and blade shapes, paddle and U-shapes, cones and stars, and balls and bones, if preferred.

PALETTE KNIVES

A long palette knife is essential for flat icing a cake with royal icing and it is also useful for sliding under and lifting delicate fondant cut-outs off a board onto a cake. For most other work, such as spreading buttercream or working joins in marzipan and fondant icing together, a flat round-ended tea or butter knife would do just as well, as long as it has a smooth and not serrated or patterned edge.

PAPER/CLING FILM/PLASTIC BAGS

Use greaseproof paper for lining tins, cutting large templates and making piping bags (see page 25). Non-stick baking paper can be used instead of greaseproof, and also as a base for making run-outs and small fondant decorations to be removed and positioned on the cake when dry. Brown wrapping paper is needed to cover the outside of cake tins when cooking rich fruit cakes to prevent overbrowning (see page 7).

Cling film can be used to cover bowls of royal icing and to wrap marzipan and fondant icing to prevent drying out. Small polythene bags are also useful for wrapping icing.

Thin card or thick paper is needed for cutting out templates, and for forming folded pieces to support drying fondant icing sections. Absorbent kitchen towel is handy to blot brushes when painting cakes, and scraps of white cartridge paper are helpful for trying out colour shades before applying the icing.

PIPING TUBES AND BAGS

Although there is a wide range of piping tubes available from kitchenware and department stores, the most useful to have are those for straight lines, writing tubes which range from very fine (No. 00) to large (No. 4 or even No. 5 in some makes), and stars, also in various sizes and numbers of points. No. 1 and No. 2 writing tubes are good ones to start with. However a paper piping bag can be cut for piping straight lines and small dots in small quantities on most informal or novelty cakes (see page 25), so even these are not immediately essential.

Try not to let icing dry in piping tubes (put them in a cup of warm water immediately after use to keep the icing soft) and clean them carefully with a small brush to prevent distortion of the shape.

Nylon piping bags are better to use with larger quantities of icing of one colour but home-made greaseproof paper bags are much easier for many different colours. They can be thrown away rather than washed and can be used without tubes.

ROLLING PIN

A long (48 cm/19 inch) heavy wooden rolling pin is best for successful rolling out of marzipan and fondant icing. Make sure too that you have a large flat surface to roll out on. Small 15 cm (6 inch) rolling pins are available for rolling out small pieces of fondant, but a small straight glass bottle (like a lemon juice bottle) would work well.

TURNTABLE

Although essential for delicate icing work, this item is a luxury for the novelty cake decorator. It is a very useful item for moving the cake around quickly to decorate different areas, but if you stand the cake on an upturned plate smaller than the size of the board, you can get your fingers underneath to turn it round.

OTHER USEFUL ITEMS

A flour shaker filled with icing sugar for dusting the work surface works very well, but you could easily use a sieve or clean tea-strainer. A pastry brush is best for applying apricot glaze. Pencils, scissors, a long ruler, string or tape measure, a set square and masking tape are all useful items.

Basic Techniques

MAKING AND COVERING CAKE BOARDS

Silver cake drums (approximately 1 cm/½ inch thick) and thinner cake boards are available in squares and circles from department stores and some stationers. Specialist cake decorating shops (see page 166 for a list) stock a whole range of sizes and shapes.

If a colour other than silver is required, the paper can easily be peeled off the boards (wet any stubborn bits with a damp cloth and they will come off) and they can then be cut to a special size if needed and covered with special cake board foil (available from specialist shops, see page 166) or any other greaseproof paper or plastic so that the oil in the cake does not mark it. Other foils and foil papers are suitable and can be simply glued onto the board and wrapped round it. Alternatively, you can use sticky-backed plastic which is available in a wide range of designs and colours from department and hardware stores. Other papers can be used and then covered in clear sticky-backed plastic to create a good effect.

Other non-flexible boards such as thick hardboard, softboard and chipboard can be cut to size and covered for cake decorating use, but it is best to cover the top and front surfaces with thin cardboard first for a smoother surface.

If you are in any doubt about the suitability of your chosen surface for food use, cut a piece of greaseproof paper slightly smaller than the size of the cake to fit under it and to protect it from the surface of the board.

PREPARING CAKE TINS

To bake a cake with a smooth, even finish – essential for cake covering and decorating – lining and greasing of cake tins is important.

The lining paper used should be greaseproof, parchment or non-stick baking paper. The paper needs to be packed well into the tin for a smooth edge, and is best made double thickness for greater insulation and easy removal. For greasing, use butter, margarine or oil. Your fingers or a pastry brush are best for applying to ensure a light but even spreading. Make sure that all corners of the cake tin are greased well.

Use the following techniques for lining tins for quick sponge cakes, and for rich fruit cakes. Victoria sponge cake is so light that you do not need to line the tins, but a circle or square of paper cut to fit the bottom of the tin will ensure an easy turn-out. Otherwise, lightly grease the tin and then dust with flour and or caster sugar. Rich fruit cake also needs a double thickness of brown paper wrapped round the outside of the tin.

Lining a round tin

1 Place the cake tin base down on a sheet of paper (double thickness if needed), and draw around it with a pencil. Cut out the circle just inside the marked line (to allow for the thickness of the tin).

2 To line the sides of the cake tin you need to cut a strip of paper (or two, for double thickness), as long as the circumference of the tin – allowing a little for overlap – and about 1 cm (½ inch) wider than its depth. (Note: The circumference is approximately three times the diameter.) Fold up one side of the strip's length to a depth of 1 cm (½ inch) and make little cuts along the length up to the folded line.
3 Press the strip around the inside of the tin so that the snipped edge tucks neatly around the base, overlapping to allow the paper to curve. Press the circles of paper into the base of the tin.
4 Lightly grease the entire surface of the paper.

Lining a square or loaf tin

1 Place the cake tin on the paper (double thickness if necessary) with its base down, and draw around the edges with a pencil. Cut out the rectangle or square just inside the marked line allowing for the thickness of the tin.
2 To line the sides of the cake tin, cut a strip as long as the combined edges of the tin (allow a little for the overlap) and about 1 cm (½ inch) wider than the cake tin's depth. Measure the length of the strip by placing the tin on the paper and turning it over four times. With a pencil, mark each corner of the tin on the paper.

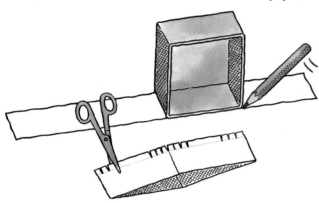

3 Fold the strip along its length where the corners occur so that you have a sharp, straight crease for each corner of the tin. Unwrap the strip. Then, fold up the length of the strip to a depth of 1 cm (½ inch) and make snips up to this folded line at the large corner creases.
4 Press the strip around the inside of the tin so that it fits neatly into the square or loaf tin. The bottom fold will overlap at the corners so that the paper fits in snugly. Make sure that the paper is pressed well into each corner. Press in the base paper and grease the inside of the tin.

Lining a pudding basin or a mixing bowl

1 Brush the sides of the basin with grease and line the bottom only with the paper by cutting out a circle of paper about 5 cm (2 inches) larger than the base of the bowl. Make 5 cm (2 inch) cuts into this paper circle all the way round.
2 Press the paper circle into the base of the bowl so that the cuts overlap the sides and it fits the base snugly. Grease the paper.

Lining an empty food can

1 Remove the wrapping label from the can and carefully remove the top with a can opener. Wash and dry the can well.
2 To line the can, cut out a rectangle of paper as long as the circumference of the can and as wide as its depth. Leave 1 cm (½ inch) on each side for overlap, and wrap the paper inside the can. Grease well.
3 To line the base, place the can on a piece of paper and draw round it. Cut out the circle, 1 cm (½ inch) outside the line, and make cuts into the circle to a depth of 1 cm (½ inch) all the way round. Grease and press down into the tin so that the snipped pieces fold up around the sides of the tin.

COVERING CAKE WITH MARZIPAN

It is important to cover a fruit cake with marzipan to prevent the icing from being stained by the cake. It also makes a smooth base for icing. Roll the marzipan out on an icing sugar dusted surface. Apricot jam can be used straight from the jar to attach marzipan to straightforward shapes if you can't be bothered to make apricot glaze; just spread it thinly with a knife avoiding any bits of fruit (cheap jam does not have much whole fruit in it). Allow at least 24 hours for the marzipan to dry before covering it with icing.

If necessary, trim the cake to level it a little and position upside down on the cake board so that you will be decorating the flat bottom of the cake. Fill any gaps around the bottom edge of the cake with small pieces of marzipan, pressing them in with a knife and holding the blade flat against the side of the cake.

To cover a round cake

Measure round the cake with a tape measure or piece of string, and measure the depth. Using about two-thirds of the marzipan, roll out and cut out a long strip using your measurements. Brush the sides of the cake with apricot glaze and attach the marzipan strip around the cake, smoothing the join together with the flat of a knife blade. This strip can be made in two pieces if preferred.

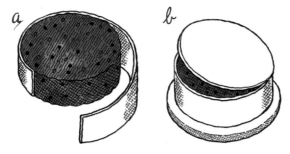

Gather together any offcuts, add them to the remaining piece of marzipan and roll into a ball. Roll this flat until a circle is formed large enough to cover the top of the cake. Brush the top of the cake with apricot glaze. Lift the marzipan onto the cake and roll the top lightly with a rolling pin to flatten it; trim off any excess round the edge with a sharp knife.

To cover a square cake

Measure the depth and length of one side. Using about a third of the marzipan, roll out and cut two strips using your measurements; brush two opposite sides of the cake with apricot glaze and attach these strips. Measure the length of one uncovered side of the cake (it will be longer than the first measurement because of the thickness of the marzipan on each side of the cake). Using a further third of the marzipan, roll out, cut out and attach strips to other sides.

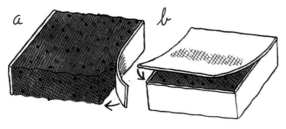

Measure the top of the cake. Gather up any offcuts, add them to the final third of the marzipan to form a ball and roll out and cut out a square to fit the top of the cake. Brush the top of the cake with apricot glaze and lift the marzipan on. Roll over lightly with a rolling pin and trim the edges with a sharp knife if necessary.

To cover an odd-shaped cake

Oval cakes can be covered in the same way as a round one, and rectangles and hexagons like a square. Odd-shaped and sculpted cakes are best covered in one piece, brushing the whole cake with apricot glaze and rolling the marzipan out to an area large enough to completely cover it. Lay the marzipan over and smooth down with your hands, easing into the shape of the cake.

COVERING CAKE WITH FONDANT ICING

Fondant icing can be used to cover sponge cakes (using apricot glaze to attach it) or to cover fruit cakes on top of marzipan (a little water brushed onto the marzipan will help the icing stick to the vertical surfaces).

1 Roll out the fondant on an icing sugar dusted board. To achieve a neat sharp-edged cake, apply the fondant icing in sections as you would marzipan, working joins together with fingers and smoothing all over with icing smoothers.

2 For a softer shape, or a sculpted cake, roll out the fondant icing in one piece until it is large enough to cover the cake, then lift it over the cake, supporting it on the rolling pin to help you if it is a large piece. Smooth the icing down over the cake with your hands and, if necessary, cut off any folds and smooth the resulting joins together with your fingers.

COVERING CAKE WITH ROYAL ICING

Covering a cake with royal icing is both tricky and time-consuming, but the finished cake has a sharp architectural quality not easily achieved with fondant icing.

Allow plenty of time to cover a cake in this way – you will need two or three coats to achieve a good finish, each of which needs at least 24 hours to dry. You can also further improve the look by icing the top of the cake one day and the sides the next or even over two days. Clearly it can be a week's job at least, possibly a fortnight!

The icing should be soft enough so that a point pulled up with the tip of a knife just turns over. If it stays up, thin the icing with a little egg white; if it will not peak at all, beat in some icing sugar.

Although you can improvise a turntable with an upturned plate, a real turntable makes the job much easier. You will also need a palette knife, a flat straight-edged icing scraper if possible, an icing ruler and a sharp knife and fine sandpaper.

1 Place the marzipan-covered cake on its board on the turntable. Put about one third of the icing on top of the cake and, using a palette knife, spread it evenly over the surface of the cake, taking care to eliminate air bubbles.

2 Using an icing ruler, the edge of an icing smoother or a long palette knife, and without pressing too hard, smooth straight across the icing towards you in even sweeps and in one direction only. Do not worry if there is still some unevenness at this stage.

3 Trim any surplus icing from the edge of the cake with a clean palette knife. If you have time, leave the cake to dry at this stage for 24 hours and then trim the rough edges with a sharp knife and rub smooth with fine sandpaper. Otherwise, proceed to cover the sides with royal icing, taking care not to disturb the top.

4 For a round cake, spread the remaining two-thirds of the icing all around the side, using a palette knife as before. Hold a smooth-edged icing scraper or ruler with one hand against the side at an angle and, turning the turntable with the other hand, pull the scraper or ruler over the side to smooth the icing. Trim away any excess icing around the top of the cake.

5 For a square or hexagonal cake, apply the icing to one side at a time, smoothing with a scraper or ruler and turning the cake each time. Apply the icing if possible to opposite sides in pairs, allowing one pair (or in the case of the hexagonal cake, three alternate sides) to dry completely before icing the other. This is to avoid touching wet sides and marking them – but this doesn't matter too much if you are putting heavy decoration along the edges later.

6 Once the icing is dry (at least 24 hours), smooth down any roughness with fine sandpaper or a sharp knife as before. Then repeat for the further layers of royal icing – the first layer will be quite thin, but following layers will smooth it out. Do not sand the final coat.

7 To cover the board, which gives a professional looking finish, spread an even layer of icing over the board with a palette knife. Using a smooth scraper or a palette knife held at an angle, draw off the icing as before to smooth the surface. Leave the finished cake to dry for at least 24 hours before decorating.

COLOURING AND PAINTING

There are many different types of food colours available and several are used in this book so here is a rundown.

Liquid colours

These are most commonly available in grocers and supermarkets, and in a wider range of colours from specialist cake decorating shops (listed on page 166). Some health food shops sell a range of food colours derived from natural sources.

Good for colouring royal and glacé icing and buttercream. Also good for colouring the basic sponge cake mixture. Add the colour to the bowl of icing a drop at a time, using a drinking straw dipped into the bottle, a teaspoon, or with a dropper if the bottle has one to apply the colour. Stir it in well until the desired shade is achieved. As liquid colour dries darker, be careful when making light colours of icing. Colour only half the quantity of icing at first so that the remainder can be added to lighten the colour if it has become too dark.

Can be used to paint light washes of colour on icing with a brush, but care must be taken not to make the icing too wet or it will become soft and lose its finish. It is also possible to colour fondant icing and marzipan light shades with liquid colours, but again these can become too wet and unmanageable if too much is added.

Not good for colouring fondant icing and marzipan dark shades.

Paste colours

Used most in this book, these colours are becoming more available in kitchen shops and can be bought from specialist shops in a large range of shades (see page 166).

Good for colouring fondant icing and marzipan and for painting onto icing and marzipan.

To add the colour to fondant icing or marzipan, make a dent in the lump of icing, add the colour (removing it from the jar with a cocktail stick), fold the icing up around the colour and knead it well in. Cut the lump of icing in half with a knife to check that it is completely mixed in and add more colour if necessary. Try to avoid making air bubbles in the icing while kneading it.

A marbled effect can be achieved by not kneading the colour in thoroughly; or by dividing the icing up, colouring it two or three different shades and then rolling the colours together before rolling out flat for use.

Dark colours will take a while to achieve but they tend to 'develop' with keeping (especially black), so wrap the icing or marzipan in a plastic bag or cling film for a while before using. A special paste called 'red compound' is good for large quantities of strong red icing; it is a brick red colour when first added to fondant but 'develops' into a rich pillar box red if wrapped and left for ten minutes or so. Dark colours will dye your hands, especially blue and green, so wear plastic gloves or be prepared to scrub your hands thoroughly.

Light colours are easy to produce but remember that the icing will dry darker, so keep back about half the quantity if you are colouring a large amount of fondant to cover a cake, so that you can lighten the shade if you have made the first part too dark; you can always add more colour but cannot subtract it.

To paint with paste colours onto royal icing, fondant icing or marzipan, make sure the surface you wish to paint on is dry. Take small amounts of the colours you wish to use from the jars using a fresh cocktail stick for each colour and put them on a white plate for a palette. Like painting with water colours, wet the brush with a little water and mix the colours on the plate. Test the colours on a sheet of white paper before painting onto the cake. Do not use the brush too wet or it will spoil the icing and the colours will run into each other. Absorbent kitchen towel is useful to blot the brush on.

Since they are translucent when painted, paste colours will be affected by the colour of icing they are painted on, so a white icing surface is best. Opaque white paste can be painted over mistakes or mixed with other paste colours to produce a thick opaque colour that is less affected by the background colour.

Can be used to colour small quantities of royal or glacé icing.

Not good for colouring *large* amounts of royal or glacé icing, because it does not mix in well and may leave dots of unmixed colour in the finished icing.

Lustre powder

Available from specialist shops (listed on page 166), these pearly colours can be rubbed or brushed dry onto dry icing to give a light sheen, or can be mixed with water to make a thick paste and painted onto dry icing to produce a rich pearly, or especially in the case of gold and silver, metallic finish which is completely edible and virtually tasteless. There are other metallic liquid colours available, but while non-toxic, they are not really edible so you have to remove the pieces of icing before eating the cake. The lustre powder is much better.

Blossom tint powder

These strong powder colours are brushed dry onto icing to give the soft shades required on flowers and other delicate work where a wet food colour would damage the icing. Available from specialist shops (listed on page 166), these colours can also be used to shade small quantities of fondant icing.

Powder colours

These extremely strong colours are useful for colouring large quantities of any type of icing, in particular for producing dark colours without thinning the icing with extra liquid. In fact a very little water does need to be added to fondant icing to help this kind of colouring 'develop'. Wear plastic gloves when kneading this into fondant icing because it will dye your hands. Since their use is fairly limited, buy powder colours as needed, don't bother with a set.

A collection of natural powder colours is now available from some specialist shops (listed on page 166) for anyone worried about food additives.

PIPING TECHNIQUES

Although lines and dots are the main piping techniques used on the cakes in this book, you may want to incorporate others detailed here in your own designs. Practise piping on a clean plate before you commence decorating a cake to get the feel of it. Royal icing is mainly used for piping, and can be returned to the bowl before it starts to dry out – buttercream too can be piped but tends to become very runny and lose its shape quickly with the warmth of your hands.

You will need a few nylon piping bags if you intend to use several colours at once, so it is easier to make paper bags which can also be used without a piping tube. If a paper piping bag should split while you are using a piping tube in it, just drop the whole thing into another bag and continue piping.

To make a paper piping bag

1 Take a piece of greaseproof or non-stick paper, and cut out a 25 cm (10 inch) square. Fold in half diagonally to make a triangle shape. Bend the triangle's side corners into the centre to form a pointed cone.

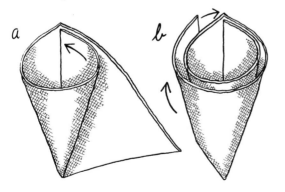

2 Fold in the overlapping corners at the top of the cone tightly to secure the end. The bag is then ready to be filled: snip off the end of the cone to the size of the hole required. This will make a double-thickness bag suitable for use with a piping tube. If you wish to just snip the end and pipe without a tube, a single thickness bag is best, so cut the square of paper in half diagonally to produce two triangles, and use just one piece.

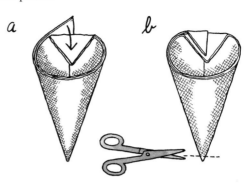

Using a piping bag

Fit the required tube into the bag and spoon in the icing until two-thirds full. Fold over the two end corners of the cone into the centre and then the top corner over this. Fold tightly.

With a large piping bag, grip it firmly so that your fingers are curled over the front of the bag and so that the folded corner is between your thumb and index finger. Press the icing out in an even line by squeezing with your hand. Keep twisting to tighten the folded ends.

If you are using a small paper bag, hold it between your middle and index finger and then push down the top with your thumb.

Piping straight lines

Hold the bag at a slight angle and press the tube on the surface. Squeeze out the icing evenly and smoothly and lift up the tube so that the icing is slightly raised – it is then easier to drop exactly into place as you go along. Try not to drag the tube along the cake as the line will look uneven. Move slowly and smoothly along the required line and stop squeezing a little before the end. Put the tube back on the surface to break off the icing and pull away neatly.

Tubes: No. 00 (very fine), No. 1 (fine), No. 2 (medium), No. 3 (thick), No. 4 (very thick).

Piping stars or rosettes

To pipe stars or rosettes, hold the icing bag at right angles to the surface with the tube just a short distance away. Squeeze gently to press out a star of icing, release and pull away the tube tip so that the icing star forms a point and breaks off. For a row of stars, pipe a row of alternate stars first, allow to dry and then fill in the gaps with some more stars.

Tubes: No. 5 (very small), No. 7 (small), No. 9 (medium), No. 11 (large), No. 12 (very large). Alternative tubes are: No. 15 (very large with more points), No. 13 (very large with more points and a fine ridged effect), and rope tubes Nos. 42, 43 and 44 (small ridged stars). Nos. 27 and 31 also make attractive small stars.

Piping shells

Shells can be made with the star tubes as detailed above but are slightly longer when piped. Squeeze out a star, pull the bag to the side to pull the star into a tail (for a shellshape), and break off.

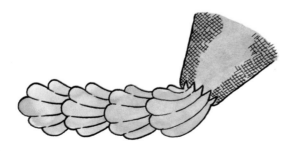

Tubes: star tubes, e.g. No. 5 (very small), No. 7 or 8 (small), No. 11 (large), No. 13 (very large).

Piping ropes

For a twisted rope effect, pipe the icing in a straight line but twist the bag as you pipe, still keeping an even pressure. Thick, ribbed or thin ropes can be created depending on the tube chosen. For very simple stranded ropes, use a plain writing tube.

Tubes: No. 42 (very small), No. 43 (small), No. 44 (medium), No. 52 (very large).

Piping basket-weave

To create this effect use a plain writing tube and a basket-weave tube. Pipe evenly spaced vertical lines over the required area with the writing tube. Change to the basket-weave tube and pipe horizontal bands across the vertical lines. Pipe down one vertical line at a time, leaving even gaps in between. Then pipe across the next vertical line so that the bands alternate with the other bands in a criss-cross fashion all the way down. Repeat all over the area to be covered.

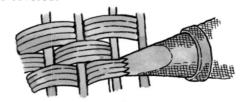

Tubes: plain writing (No. 1 or No. 2) and basket-weave (No. 22 or No. 48).

TEMPLATES

Various kinds of templates and tracings are used in this book to transfer a chosen design onto a cake, as a guide to cutting unusual shapes that need to be repeated several times, or merely to help pipe lines or dots at regular intervals onto a cake. Tracing or greaseproof paper are necessary and other useful items are thin card, pencils, a ruler, and, for geometric shapes, other drawing instruments, scissors and pins.

1 To transfer a design onto a cake as a guide for painting: lay a sheet of tracing or greaseproof paper over the design and trace the outline in pencil. Turn the paper over and go over the lines with a soft pencil, turn back and lay the paper on the area of icing to be painted. Hold the tracing steady with one hand and go over the lines on the paper again with a pencil, pressing lightly onto the icing. Remove the paper to reveal the soft pencilled outline on the icing.

2 To transfer a design onto a cake as a guide to piping: trace the design onto tracing or grease-proof paper with a pencil. Place the paper on the icing to be decorated. Hold it steady with one hand and with a pin prick the outline through the paper into the icing. Remove the paper and pipe over the outline with icing to cover the tiny holes.

3 To make a template as a guide for cut-outs: trace the design from the book onto tracing or grease-proof paper. Turn over, place on thin card or thick paper and go over the lines on the back of the paper with a pencil to trace the design down. Remove the paper and cut out the card shape with scissors. Turn the card template over to make it the right way round. Alternatively, if you are confident, draw the shape freehand onto the card and cut out. Place the template on the icing to be cut out, hold with one hand and cut round with a sharp knife.

4 To make a template as a guide for piping: if you wish to pipe, for example, a row of dots at regular intervals on a cake, cut a strip of paper or card the same length or shape as the required line of dots and mark on the edge where you want the dots to go, using a ruler to measure the spacing. Hold or just place the template on the cake near where you want the icing to go and pipe close to its edge, following your marks.

MAKING RUN-OUTS

This technique is used to make a smooth solid area of royal icing in an exact shape, piped directly onto a cake or as a separate piece on non-stick or waxed paper to be removed when dry and then attached to a cake. The basic method is quite simple to learn – the outline of a shape is piped with royal icing (see page 14), filled in with thinned royal icing to 'flood' the shape and then left flat to dry.

Run-out pieces made on non-stick or waxed paper are delicate and brittle but self-support-ing, so they can be used to build out a design from the surface of a cake if carefully attached with royal icing. Quite open lacework pieces can be made in the same way without filling in with thinned icing, and they can even be dried over a rolling pin into a curve. It is also possible to make quite complex coloured run-outs by piping and filling the adjoining areas in different colours. Strong colours can often leach into lighter ones so bear this in mind when planning your design.

1 To make a run-out on waxed or non-stick paper, pencil your design on a piece of paper (several times is advisable, in case of breakages) and tape it down firmly onto a board. Place a sheet of paper over and secure with masking tape.

2 Using royal icing and a fine plain writing tube (No. 1 or 2), pipe a thin, even line around the outline of the shape through the paper.

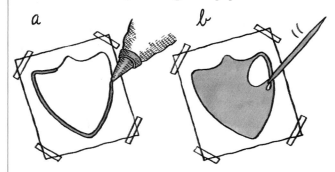

3 The icing used for flooding the inside of the shape needs to be slightly runnier in consist-ency, so mix in a little unbeaten egg white or water, a drop at a time, until you reach a cream-like consistency. Using a teaspoon or a paper piping bag with a large hole snipped in the end of it, gradually spoon or pipe the thinner icing into the centre of the shape. Using a cocktail stick, gradually take the icing out to the piped edging line until all the corners are filled.

4 Prick any air bubbles with a cocktail stick if they occur. The shape should be quite full with a smooth, sheer surface.

5 Leave the run-out to set completely, and do not attempt to remove it from the paper for at least 24 hours. Large run-outs can take even longer to dry out. Attach the finished run-out to the cake with a dab of royal icing.

bROADWAY BABIES

Another Folly, but this time of the Ziegfeld kind, celebrating those musical variety extravaganzas that featured regiments of leggy lovelies dancing or just posed around spectacular sets in wonderful line-ups and kaleidoscopic patterns – the trademark of choreographer Busby Berkeley.
You may like to make more girls, girls, girls to decorate your cake or go wild with more tiers of cake and grander costumes.

INGREDIENTS

quantity for 25 cm (10 inch) square rich fruit cake, divided between a 25 × 20 cm (10 × 8 inch) oval tin and a 15 × 10 cm (6 × 4 inch) oval tin (p.7)

apricot glaze (p.17)

1.2 kg (2 lb 11 oz) marzipan (p.15)

1.8 kg (4 lb) fondant icing (p.15)

icing sugar for dusting

basic paste food colours: violet, pink, black, yellow, red

225 g (8 oz) royal icing (p.14)

silver balls

OTHER MATERIALS

30 × 25 cm (12 × 10 inch) oval cake board (drum)

20 × 15 cm (8 × 6 inch) oval cake board (drum)

six 7.5 cm (3 inch) round silver tapered pillars

4 cocktail sticks

SPECIAL EQUIPMENT

piping bag with No. 3 writing tube

scissors

piece of scrap paper

saucer

turntable (if possible)

baked bean tin

small round cutter

paper piping bag

fine artist's paint brush

NOTE: Allow at least 1 day extra preparation time for marzipan to dry.

1 Trim the tops of the cakes level and turn them over so you can decorate the flat bases. Position the large cake slightly off centre on the larger cake board and the small cake to one side of the smaller cake board. Brush with apricot glaze and cover both cakes with marzipan in the same way as a round cake (p.21), using 900 g (2 lb) for the large cake and 300 g (11 oz) for the small one. Leave to dry for at least 24 hours.

2 Colour 850 g (1 lb 14 oz) of the fondant lilac and use to cover the round cakes in the same way as with the marzipan: roll the fondant out on an icing sugar dusted surface and attach round the sides of the cakes with a little water if necessary. Work the joins together with your fingers or use a flat-bladed knife. Use 500 g (1 lb 2 oz) to cover the large cake and 250 g (9 oz) to cover the small one. Using the remaining lilac fondant, roll out thin strips to cover the cake boards, butting right up to the sides of the cakes and trimming off neatly. Smooth the joins together and leave the cakes to dry for a couple of hours.

3 Place a third of the royal icing in the piping bag with a No. 3 writing tube. Cut a small

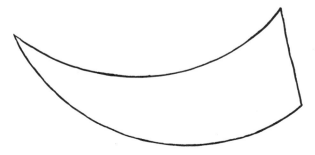

curved template from scrap paper and using this as a guide, pipe small dots at regular intervals in curved lines around the boards and up the back of both cakes, stopping every six dots or so to press a silver ball into each one. A turntable will make this job quicker and easier.

4 Colour 500 g (1 lb 2 oz) more of the fondant flesh-pink, reserve 200 g (7 oz) of it (tightly wrapped) and add a little black to the rest to give a slightly duller shade. Stand the smaller cake on a baked bean tin. Divide the dull pink fondant into seven pieces, and from each piece roll two shapely sausages for each pair of legs. Position three pairs around the front of the smaller cake board and three around the front of the larger cake; re-wrap the last piece to make the top figure later. Press all the legs onto the drum or cake to secure. You may wish to assemble the cake briefly with the columns in place to check the positioning of the lower figures to ensure that the top ones won't be kicking them.

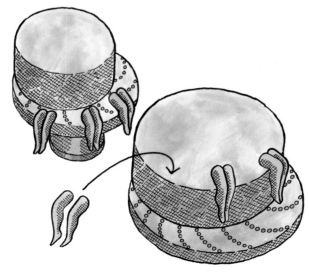

5 Colour 425 g (15 oz) of the fondant black. Dampen the cocktail sticks with a little water and push them a little way into the cakes where the bodies are going to go, three in the large cake and one on the very top of the small cake. (The figures seated around the side of the smaller cake do not need cocktail sticks as they lean against the cake.) Roughly press a small piece of black fondant around each stick to give a small base for the figures and dry for about 1 hour.

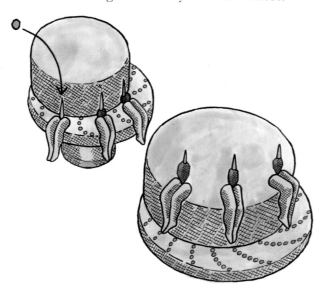

6 Divide the remaining black fondant into eight and reserve one of these pieces, tightly wrapped, to make the hats later. Starting with the figures on the small cake, make a pair of shoes from each piece of black fondant, attaching them to the bottom of the legs with a little water. Next make a torso for each figure, pressing it into place against the side of the cake. Make the three figures for the large cake and the figure on the top by pressing the fondant into torsos around the covered cocktail sticks. Make a pair of legs for the top figure from the reserved dull pink fondant and stick in place, remembering to make a pair of black fondant shoes for her feet.

7 Roll out the remaining white fondant thinly on an icing sugar dusted surface and, with a sharp knife, cut out seven bibs and attach them to the figures with a little water. Gather up the offcuts and make seven small discs with a section cut out of each, and attach to each figure to make a collar.

8 Divide the reserved flesh-pink fondant into seven and from each piece make two small sausages for arms and a ball for the head, pinching out a nose shape with your fingers. Attach to each torso with a little water.

9 Roll out a little of the remaining black fondant on an icing sugar dusted surface, cut out seven circles for the hat brims and seven bow ties. Position with a little water on the cakes, placing the hat brims on the laps of the girls, except for the very top girl who is wearing her hat on her head. Roll out the rest of the black fondant into a thick sausage and cut off seven short lengths to make the tops of the hats.

10 Colour half of the remaining royal icing yellow, place in a paper piping bag and snip a small hole at the end. Pipe the hair in rough blobs under the brim of the hat of the top figure and all over the other heads.

11 Place the remaining white royal icing in a clean piping bag with a No. 3 writing tube and, as in step 3, pipe dots and stick on silver balls around the top figure, the top edge of the cakes, between the figures and anywhere else that looks bare or boring!

12 With a fine artist's paint brush and black food colouring, paint eyes and eyebrows onto the faces, and with the red colouring paint their lips. Thin red colouring with water and paint on to redden the cheeks.

13 Assemble the cakes into tiers, placing the pillars upside down (widest part at the top) to give a real 1930s Hollywood feel.

CAKE ON TAP

A champagne bottle is a common subject for a cake but a beer or lager drinker would surely prefer to celebrate with a pint. Soak half of the cake fruit in beer for an hour before using (leave out the brandy in the recipe) to give an extra moist cake.

Four-star lager is an invention of mine (sounds more like petrol!) so you could copy a favourite brand or use the recipient's name as part of the design. I have made this cake before for a publican's wedding using linked hearts and initials as the motif, and with a larger square cake covered in brown fondant (to resemble a wooden bar top) for the bottom tier.

INGREDIENTS

15 cm (6 inch) square rich fruit cake (p.7)
two 882 g (1 lb 15 oz) can-shaped rich fruit cakes, using quantity for 15 cm (6 inch) round divided between each can (p.7)
apricot glaze (p.17)
600 g (1 lb 5 oz) marzipan (p.15)
icing sugar for dusting
650 g (1 lb 7 oz) fondant icing (p.15)
basic paste food colours: red, brown, yellow, blue, black
silver lustre powder
opaque white food colour

OTHER MATERIALS

18 cm (7 inch) square cake board (drum), covered with wood-effect sticky-back plastic

SPECIAL EQUIPMENT

non-stick baking paper
icing smoothers
No. 4 writing tube
small round cutters or various jars and lids
fine artist's paint brush

NOTE: Allow at least 1 day extra preparation time for marzipan to dry.

1 Trim the 15 cm (6 inch) square cake level then cut all four sides at an angle as shown in the diagram. Cut the tops of the two can-shaped cakes level and sandwich them together with apricot glaze and a circle of 25 g (1 oz) marzipan rolled out on an icing sugar dusted surface. Carve this cylinder of cake so that it tapers down towards the bottom. Brush the 'square' cake with apricot glaze.

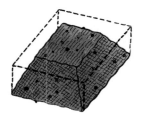

2 Position the square cake towards the back of the cake board and cover with 250 g (9 oz) of the marzipan as you would cover a square cake (p.22).

3 Measure round the cylinder cake at its widest point and its height. Roll out 300 g (11 oz) marzipan to an area slightly larger than these dimensions. Brush with glaze, then place the cake on the marzipan and roll up. Trim off any excess and work together the join with the flat blade of a knife. Roll the covered cake around on an icing sugar dusted surface to achieve a smooth finish. Stand the cake on a piece of non-stick baking paper; roll out any trimmings and the remaining marzipan to a circle to fit the top of the cake, attach and neaten the join. Leave both the square and the cylindrical cake to dry for at least 24 hours.

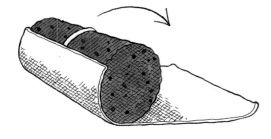

4 Colour 200 g (7 oz) fondant red and roll out on an icing sugar dusted surface to an approximate 30 cm (12 inch) square. Lift over the square cake, smooth down all round and trim off any excess at the corners and bottom. Reserve these trimmings for decorations.

5 Colour 250 g (9 oz) fondant golden-brown. Make a sausage from 50 g (2 oz) of it to fit round the cylindrical cake near the top. Flatten it onto the cake to make the bump in the glass.

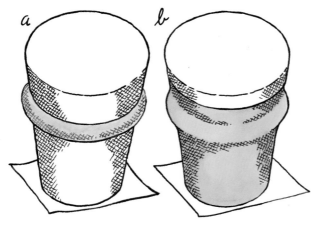

6 Turn the cake upside down on a fresh piece of non-stick paper and dampen it all over with a little water on your fingers. Roll out the remaining 200 g (7 oz) golden-brown fondant to a large rectangle and wrap round the cake. Trim away the fondant about 1 cm (½ inch) from the bottom – the actual top of the cake – in a straight line. Turn the cake the right way up.

7 Make a ball of 50 g (2 oz) white fondant, roll it into a flat circle to fit the top of the cake, position on and smooth together where it joins round the edge. Press a large writing tube (No. 4) all over the top for the air bubbles.

8 Take 25 g (1 oz) of white fondant and roll out to a strip of the same thickness as the golden-brown, about 1 cm (½ inch) wide and long enough to fit round the top of the cake. Fix it round the top of the cake, butting it up to the golden-brown fondant and smoothing together the join at the back.

9 Roll 25 g (1 oz) of white fondant to a long thin sausage and attach with a little water round the top of the cake to make the glass rim.

10 Divide the remaining fondant in three and colour one piece blue, one black and one grey. Together with the red offcuts, roll each colour out and use to make the design on the front of the glass and stand; using cutters and a pointed knife, cut the required shapes out of the coloured fondant. Then, cut out the same shapes from the front of the cake glass and stand and pull away the golden-brown and red fondant. Insert the design pieces into these holes on the cake, smoothing the surfaces firmly together. Mould the stars on the base cake from grey fondant, fix them on with a little water and again paint with silver lustre powder mixed with a little water. Paint stars onto the glass with opaque white food colouring, leave to dry for a short time and then paint over with silver lustre powder mixed with a little water.

11 To serve, remove the glass cake from the non-stick paper and position on top of the base cake. You may need to press in the red fondant on the base cake to get it level. If you wish to leave the cakes together for more than 24 hours it is best to leave a small circle of non-stick paper on the bottom of the glass cake to prevent the fruit cake underneath from staining the red fondant.

*d*ISH OF THE DAY

Commemorative plates have for a long time been a good way to mark special events, births, anniversaries and coronations, and this one is inspired by the design of 17th-century English delftware. The shape will depend on the kind of dinner plate you have available as a mould and a sift through a few books at the local library will provide you with plenty of designs to decorate it. You may like to tint the fondant icing to give the plate a background colour but remember that this will affect the colours you paint on as they are fairly transparent. As a variation on this design, make the basic plate a terracotta colour and decorate it with royal icing for an ethnic-style plate – an appropriate gift for a potter.

INGREDIENTS
20 cm (8 inch) round rich fruit cake (p.7)
icing sugar for dusting
750 g (1 lb 10 oz) fondant icing (p.15)
apricot glaze (p.17)
500 g (1 lb 2 oz) marzipan (p.15)
basic paste food colours: violet, red, light blue, dark blue, brown, orange, green, or colours of choice
small amount of royal icing (p.14)

OTHER MATERIALS
28 cm (11 inch) round cake board

SPECIAL EQUIPMENT
non-stick baking paper
25 cm (10 inch) round dinner plate
absorbent kitchen paper
large flat board
artist's paint brushes

NOTE: Allow at least 4 days extra preparation time for icing to set and 2 hours for food colours to dry.

1 Cut two strips of non-stick baking paper about 2.5 cm (1 inch) wide and at least 38 cm (15 inches) long, and lay them across the dinner plate (see diagram). Dredge the plate thoroughly with icing sugar.

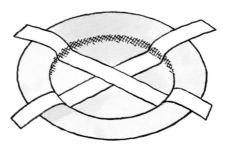

2 On a surface dredged with icing sugar, roll out 400 g (14 oz) of the fondant icing into a circle slightly larger than the dinner plate and carefully lift it onto the plate, easing it into the shape and trimming the edges with a sharp knife. Dust your hands with icing sugar and smooth the icing all over. Leave to dry for at least 24 hours.

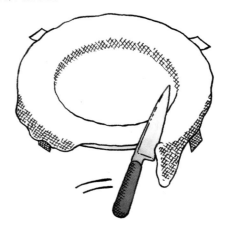

3 Make a small pad of kitchen paper wrapped in non-stick baking paper (to support the middle of the hardened icing) and place in the centre of the icing plate. Cover with a 28 cm (11 inch) square piece of non-stick baking paper and a large flat tray. Upturn the whole thing and use the non-stick baking paper strips to ease off the dinner plate. Leave at least another 24 hours to dry on the non-stick paper.

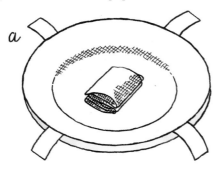

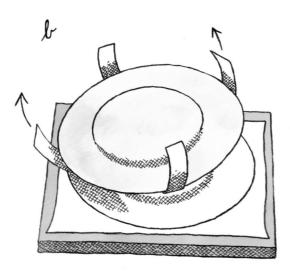

4 Dredge the back of the upturned icing plate thoroughly with icing sugar, fit the dinner plate back on and turn over again. Leave for a further 24 hours to dry.

The next two steps can be done, if preferred, after painting the plate.

5 Trim the rough top of the fruit cake at a slight angle (you will be using the cake right way up) and position it on the cake board so that it slopes towards the front. Spread the cake thinly with apricot glaze and cover the top and sides with the marzipan in the same way as a regular round cake (p.21), trimming the side strips where the sides of the cake are uneven. Leave to dry for at least 24 hours.

6 Colour the remaining fondant icing violet. Using two-thirds of it, roll out on an icing sugar dusted surface two strips, each 14 cm (5½ inches) wide and 32 cm (12½ inches) long (half the circumference of the cake). Apply the strips firmly around the cake, ensuring a neat fit at the board and smoothing together the joins. Fold the excess over the top of the cake and smooth down. Roll out the remaining fondant fairly thin and cut into strips to cover the cake board, joining and butting them up to the sides of the cake. Trim neatly and leave the cake and board to dry until needed.

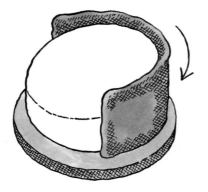

7 Plan your plate design and lightly trace or pencil it freehand onto the icing plate (which is still on the dinner plate). Remember that heavy pencil marks will smudge and show through lighter colours. Thin the paste colours a little with water, using another plate as a palette, and using a fairly dry brush, paint the design onto the icing plate. Have a sheet of paper handy to test the shade and consistency of the various colours, and kitchen paper to blot the brush.

Once painted, leave the plate to dry for a couple of hours.

8 Cover the icing plate with a sheet of non-stick baking paper and a large flat board, upturn and remove the dinner plate, brushing off any excess icing sugar on the bottom. Carefully pick up the icing plate, turn it over and attach it to the top of the fruit cake with a blob of royal icing.

_t_HE PERSISTENCE OF MEMORY

I suppose the ideal birthday cake for a surrealist might be a live lobster or a grand piano complete with candelabra. This cake is perhaps better suited to someone who just enjoys looking at surrealist art, especially the work of the Spanish artist Salvador Dali, on one of whose paintings this cake design is based.

While his idea of a soft watch is now familiar (Dali said that his love of Camembert cheese inspired the shape), the tiny fondant ants will hopefully elicit just a little of the shocked reaction that the original painting must have produced when it was first shown in the early 1930s – before mass exposure to Dali's images in the media (especially in advertising) made people immune to their disturbing dreamlike qualities.

INGREDIENTS

20 cm (8 inch) square sponge cake (p.9)
raspberry jam
300 g (11 oz) buttercream (p.17)
1 kg (2 lb 4 oz) fondant icing (p.15)
basic paste food colours: brown, orange, blue, yellow, black
icing sugar for dusting

OTHER MATERIALS

23 cm (9 inch) square cake board (drum), covered with brown sticky-back plastic
suitably shaped twig

SPECIAL EQUIPMENT

cling film
apple corer
medium and fine artist's paint brushes

1 In order to obtain the flattest possible top for the finished cake, trim a little off the top of the sponge cake to level it then turn the cake upside down.

2 Cut the cake in half horizontally, spread the bottom half with jam to within 1 cm (½ inch) of the edges then spread all over with half of the buttercream. Position in one corner of the cake board and place the other half cake on top.

3 Spread a little of the remaining buttercream thinly over the top and then cover the sides, filling any holes and gaps. Aim to get the surfaces as flat and square as possible.

4 Colour 600 g (1 lb 5 oz) of the fondant a warm brown. On an icing sugar dusted surface, roll out and cut two pieces to fit the front and back sides of the cake, approximately 20 × 7.5 cm (8 × 3 inches) and 20 × 9 cm (8 × 3½ inches) – the back piece should be wide enough to cover the edge of the cake board too. Lightly press them onto the cake. Roll out and cut a large wide strip approximately 36.5 × 20 cm (14½ × 8 inches), long enough to drape over the entire cake in one piece from the base of the cake board, up the outside, over the top and down the other side to meet the board. Place this smoothly on the cake and carefully work together the joins, making sure not to get buttercream on the surface of the cake. Leave to dry.

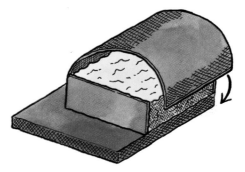

5 Clean the twig as much as possible and cover its bottom end with cling film to the depth of the cake. With a pointed knife, cut a hole in the icing on the top of the cake and carefully excavate the cake below (an apple corer may help with this). Push the twig right into the cake so that it is straight and square.

6 Colour 50 g (2 oz) of the fondant a rich orange colour. Roll a tiny ball of it to make a watch winder, marking all round the edge with a knife to give a ridged texture. Roll the rest of the orange fondant into a ball and flatten to an oval shape to make the face-down watch. Attach the winder to the top with a little water and position onto the front right corner of the cake.

7 Colour 100 g (4 oz) of the remaining fondant light blue, 50 g (2 oz) a slightly darker blue, 175 g (6 oz) yellow (you may like to use two different shades of yellow) and 25 g (1 oz) black. Make the two flat melting watches on the cake by rolling out, on an icing sugar dusted surface, two small pieces of the darker blue fondant. Cut each to a rough semi-oval shape and attach to the top of the cake butting up to the edge; roll out the light blue, cut to a drooping semi-oval shape, and attach to the side of the cake so that it meets the dark blue half. Smooth together the join.

8 Roll out two thin sausages of yellow fondant and attach one all around the edge of each blue fondant watch with a little water, working together the join at the top. Make two winders from small balls of yellow as in step 6, mark ridges all round and attach one to the top of each watch.

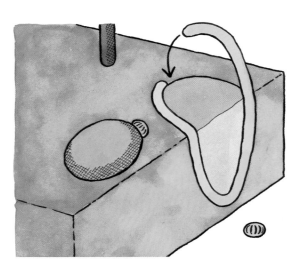

9 To make the hanging watch, roll out a piece of the yellow fondant to an elongated oval shape and hang it over the twig (press a small lump of fondant on the twig underneath the watch to support it a little). Make a winder as

before and attach it. Roll out a light blue watch face (fairly thin) and lay it over the yellow, then make a thin sausage of yellow to frame the watch as before, securing it with a little water. This is a very delicate operation, so don't worry if it takes you a few attempts.

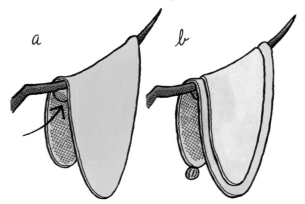

10 With the black fondant, roll out tiny thin sausage strips to make the six hands for all the watches and attach them with a dampened paint brush. Roll out very small balls of black to make each section of the ants' bodies (three sections to each) and attach them on the face-down watch with a little water.

11 Using a plate as a palette, mix shades of brown with varying amounts of water and paint the shading on the cake as shown in the photograph, creating shadows for the watches, the tree and the ants and giving form to the watches and winders.

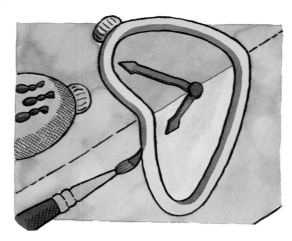

12 Finally, with a fine artist's paint brush and black colouring, paint the ants' legs and the numbers and minutes on the watches.

WISH YOU WERE HERE

This cake is based on the seaside postcard illustrations of Donald McGill. Available at British seafront kiosks in the 1930s, these postcards are now collector's items portraying a world of bloated bathers, nagging landladies and sparrow-chested, hen-pecked husbands.

As my birthday falls near August bank holiday I have celebrated quite a few on the beach. I'm also quite 'plump' in stature so perhaps this is the cake for me!

INGREDIENTS

20 cm (8 inch) square rich fruit cake (p.7)
450 ml (¾ pint) pudding basin rich fruit cake, using half the quantity for a 15 cm (6 inch) round (p.7)
1 kg (2 lb 4 oz) marzipan (p.15)
icing sugar for dusting
apricot glaze (p.17)
1.2 kg (2 lb 11 oz) fondant icing (p.15)
basic paste food colours: pink, red, brown, blue, black

OTHER MATERIALS

28 × 23 cm (11 × 9 inch) cake board (drum), cut from a 28 cm (11 inch) square and then covered with silver cake board paper
cocktail stick
wooden skewer

SPECIAL EQUIPMENT

thick skewer or pencil
spice jars
skewer or modelling tools
cocktail stick
ruler
fine artist's paint brush

NOTE: Allow at least 1 day extra preparation time for marzipan to dry.

1 Trim the square cake level and cut 4 cm (1½ inches) off one side (see diagram). Cut this thin piece down to 16 cm (6½ inches) long. Roll out 50 g (2 oz) marzipan on an icing sugar dusted surface to measure roughly 16 × 7.5 cm (6½ × 3 inches). Brush one short end of the larger piece and one long side of the small piece with apricot glaze and sandwich together with the piece of marzipan between to make an oblong cake. Position on the cake board.

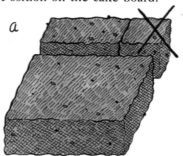

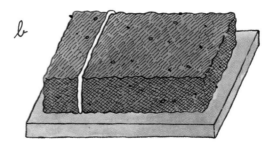

2 Cut the top of the cake at a slight angle sloping down to the front and build up the back a little with 50 g (2 oz) marzipan, moulded to a long wedge.

3 Brush the sides of the cake with apricot glaze. On an icing sugar dusted surface, roll out 300 g (11 oz) marzipan, a little at a time, into pencil-thick sausages. Flatten a little, cut to length and stick upright around all the sides of the cake spaced apart equally and making sure there is one at each corner (see diagram).

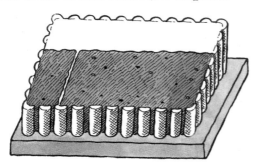

4 Roll out 250 g (9 oz) marzipan. Measure the depth of each side of the cake and cut out four strips from the marzipan to cover the sides – this is done in the same way as you would cover a square cake (p.21), but take into account the angle of the sides and that you will need approximately 50 per cent extra length to go round the bumps on the sides. Apply the marzipan pieces to the sides of the cake, pressing well into the gaps between the bumps with a thick skewer or pencil. Trim off any excess.

5 Measure then brush the top of the cake with apricot glaze. Roll out 200 g (7 oz) more marzipan roughly to size, place on top of the cake and roll lightly with a rolling pin to level it out. With a sharp knife, carefully trim round the bumpy edges, pressing the surfaces together.

6 Trim the top of the pudding basin cake level, turn upside down and carve the front of the cake a little to make the slope of the chest from the shoulders, the cleavage and top of the belly. Brush the base of the cake with apricot glaze and position it in the centre of the other cake, slightly towards the front. Brush all over with apricot glaze.

7 Build up the shoulders a little with offcuts of marzipan then roll out the remaining marzipan to a circle approximately 15 cm (6 inches) in diameter. Lay this over the pudding cake, smoothing down all round and into the curves and trimming neatly at the bottom. Leave to dry for at least 24 hours.

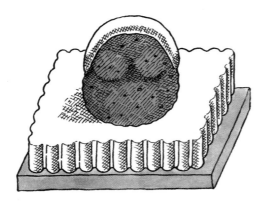

8 Push a cocktail stick into the top of the pudding cake to support the head. Break a wooden skewer in half and push a piece into each side of the cake to support the arms.

9 Colour 250 g (9 oz) of the fondant flesh-pink. Dampen the cocktail stick and skewer with a little water and then take a small piece of pink fondant and press it onto the cocktail stick to make the basis of the neck. While this is drying a little, use 75 g (3 oz) of the flesh pink fondant to mould an arm and hand all in one piece. Leave extra fondant at the shoulder end and hollow that end a little. Push the fondant arm onto one of the skewers and smooth the shoulder end onto the cake. Support the arm with spice jars or extra fondant. Repeat with a further 75 g (3 oz) pink fondant for the other arm. Allow to dry for at least 1 hour before removing the supports.

10 Meanwhile, using the remaining pink fondant, mould the head, neck and hollow upper torso in one piece, so that the head and neck can fit over the cocktail stick while the large flaps can smooth over the marzipan chest and back. Press this shape onto the cocktail stick and mould the chest and back onto the cake. Mould the features on the face with a pointed knife and a skewer or modelling tools. Add small pieces of fondant to build up the nose and cheeks, cut out the mouth and press out eye

sockets with a cocktail stick, filling them in with tiny pieces of white fondant to make eyeballs and teeth. Trim a line around the pink fondant where the swimming costume will come, and remove any excess below. Build up the shape of the bosom and belly with these offcuts, smoothing the fondant well into the marzipan base.

11 Colour 100 g (4 oz) more fondant red. On an icing sugar dusted surface, roll out this and then 100 g (4 oz) white fondant to make two rectangles, each 25 × 4 cm (10 × 1½ inches). Using a ruler and a sharp knife, cut both pieces into long thin strips approximately 1 cm (½ inch) wide. Arrange the strips, alternating the colours, on the icing sugar dusted surface and roll together to make a single striped piece.

12 Dampen the bare marzipan on the figure with a little water on your fingers and then carefully lift the red and white striped fondant onto the front of the figure making sure it is aligned neatly at the bottom. Wrap the fondant around the belly and the arms, smoothing and cutting as you go to make it fit. Trim the costume around the edges so that it butts neatly up against the flesh fondant. Use some of the offcuts to complete the stripes up the chest straps, and to tidy the join at the back. Next roll out thin sausages of the red offcuts to make border piping around the neck and arms of the costume. A little water applied with a fine brush will help this piping and other small decorations stick firmly.

13 Colour a small piece of the white fondant offcuts brown and roll tiny lengths for the hair; curl these around the head, applying with a little water. Make a hat from a rolled out piece of red fondant and a white flower with a red centre from more scraps. Reserve any remaining scraps of fondant and colour it all red for the border of the postcard picture later, keeping it tightly wrapped.

14 Colour 25 g (1 oz) fondant mid-blue and, 50 g (2 oz) pale blue. Roll these two colours together roughly into a ball and then stick a 25 g (1 oz) ball of white fondant onto one side. Roll together a little and then roll out on an icing sugar dusted surface to an area approximately 24 × 7.5 cm (9½ × 3 inches). You should get a 'cloudy sky' look but if you are not happy with it, gather the fondant up into a ball and keep rolling it out until you are. Lay this blue and white fondant over the back half of the top of the cake; using a sharp knife and ruler, cut the edges so that there is a 2 cm (¾ inch) frame all the way round the sky. Trim the sky just behind the figure in a straight line, to make the horizon appear just behind the fat lady.

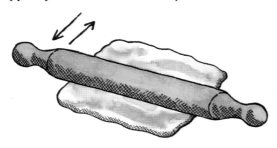

15 Gather up the fondant offcuts from the sky. Colour 150 g (5½ oz) of the remaining fondant greeny-blue then roll together with the sky offcuts. Roll out on an icing sugar dusted surface to achieve a marbled sea effect; but again if you are not happy with the pattern gather the fondant up and reroll until you are. Roll out to make two pieces large enough to fit either side of the figure allowing some extra at the inner edge to make the waves. Cut the top edge of these pieces straight to butt up to the sky area and arrange the rest in small waving folds around the figure, folding pieces back where they meet the figure to look like breaking waves. Top these waves with tiny pieces of white fondant to resemble sea foam. Trim round the edges against a ruler as with the sky.

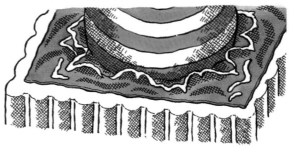

16 Make a very thin sausage of the red scraps to fit right round the 'picture' on the postcard cake, forming an inner frame. Attach with a little water applied with a brush and trim the lines straight with a knife.

17 Roll out 400 g (14 oz) of the remaining white fondant on an icing sugar dusted surface and cover the sides of the cake in the same way as you covered them with marzipan in Step 4, pressing the fondant into the dents with a pencil or skewer and trimming neatly at the top and bottom edges.

18 Roll out the remaining white fondant and cut thin strips 1 cm (½ inch) wide to form a border round the red frame on the cake. Work together any joins with your fingers then trim round the wavy edge with a sharp knife. Press the back of a knife to make horizontal lines all the the way down the rippling sides of the cake to resemble a stack of postcards.

19 With a small brush paint the features on the face, making the cheeks and nose rosy with red food colouring thinned with water.

PIGS IN MUCK

This saying usually has a rather more 'Anglo Saxon' ending but the sentiment is the same – blissful happiness on the simplest terms.
An otherwise unremarkable wedding anniversary would be greatly cheered up with this amusing cake, or you could make it for a 'sty-warming' party – a door number on a plaque hanging on the fence would be a nice touch!
A walnut whip makes a good base for moulding small figures and animals as well as being a pleasant surprise when eaten. Use white marzipan in order to achieve the best possible pink colour.

INGREDIENTS

18 cm (7 inch) round chocolate sponge cake (p.9)

400 g (14 oz) hazelnut-chocolate buttercream (p.17)

500 g (1 lb 2 oz) marzipan (p.15)

2 Walnut Whips

Matchmakers

50 g (2 oz) fondant icing (p.15)

basic paste food colours: pink, black, and other colours of choice

OTHER MATERIALS

20 cm (8 inch) round cake board (drum)

SPECIAL EQUIPMENT

skewer or cocktail stick

fine artist's paint brush

1 Split the cake in half horizontally and sandwich together with a third of the buttercream. Position in the centre of the cake board and cover the entire cake with most of the remaining buttercream – reserve a little to spread on the pigs.

2 Colour the marzipan pink. Using approximately half the marzipan, make the torsos of the pigs, moulding them carefully around the Walnut Whips to give a firm base. Reserving some marzipan for the legs and ears, roll two

pear-shaped balls for the heads and mould into the shape of pig faces: cut a slit for the mouth and form a snout with your fingers, using a skewer or cocktail stick to mould the nostrils and eyes (make eyeballs with a tiny amount of white fondant). Mould ears with a little marzipan and press on to the heads. Place the heads on the bodies; they will stick easily.

4 Push Matchmakers into the back of the cake in a row to make the fence behind the pigs, joining the cross pieces by melting them a little with a hot knife and pressing together.

3 Make the legs from small sausages of marzipan and attach (except for the one that goes round the lady pig's shoulder), to the bodies. Place the pigs onto the cake, pressing them down into the buttercream. Attach the last leg around the shoulder of the pig and smooth over the join. Spread a few bits of buttercream around the base and up the bellies of the pigs to make them look really mucky.

5 Paint features on the pigs with paste food colouring and use your imagination and plasticine-playing abilities to make clothes, accessories and streamers from small pieces of coloured fondant: roll out various colours on an icing sugar dusted surface and cut out shapes for the collar, tie, glasses (with thin sausages for the frames), small balls for beads and thin strips for streamers. Attach to the pigs with a dampened paint brush.

a HANDBAG

When I was young, we used to call one of my grannies 'Mrs Haberdashery' because she was sure to be able to produce everything but the kitchen sink from her seemingly bottomless handbag. Needle and thread, scissors, a nail file that doubled as a screwdriver, paper, pens, hankies, sweets, keys.

If you have seen anyone drop their bag (and briefcases are no exception), out spills all manner of articles related to their life, work or just irrelevant junk that happens to be there – plenty of material for a cake! Make all the pieces lifesize to avoid making them in proportion to each other and do not be afraid to make more than would fit into the bag – it could be a lot funnier.

INGREDIENTS

two 25 cm (10 inch) square shallow chocolate sponge cakes, using quantity for 20 cm (8 inch) square in each (p.9)

600 g (1 lb 5 oz) chocolate buttercream (p.17)

400 g (14 oz) chewy chocolate covering made with dark chocolate (p.16)

approximately 500 g (1 lb 2 oz) fondant icing (p.15)

icing sugar for dusting

basic paste food colours: red, yellow, black, and other colours of choice

225 g (8 oz) royal icing (p.14)

gold and silver lustre powder

silver balls, boiled sweets, chocolate coins

OTHER MATERIALS

30 cm (12 inch) square cake board, covered with pink sticky-back plastic

wooden skewers

cocktail sticks

SPECIAL EQUIPMENT

non-stick baking paper

paper piping bag (p.19)

artist's paint brushes

NOTE: Allow 1 hour extra preparation time for icing to dry.

1 Trim approximately a quarter (6.5 cm/2½ inches) off one side of each cake to make two oblong shapes.

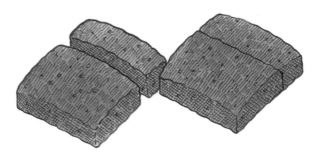

2 Place one cake upside down on the pink-covered cake board and cut away under the front and back edges to accentuate the curve of the bag. This can be done off the board if preferred.

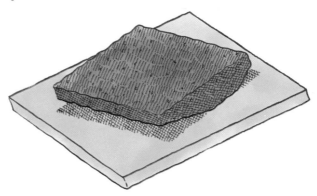

3 Cut one of the long quarter side offcuts from step 1 into a wedge and attach to the back of the cake on the board with some buttercream.

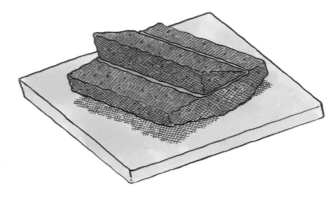

4 Holding the second cake the right way up, trim the front and back top in a similar way to form the other curved side of the handbag. Secure it on top of the first cake with more buttercream – the offcut wedge will angle it upwards to look like an open bag. Spread the whole cake, outside and inside, with the remaining buttercream.

5 Reserve 75 g (3 oz) of the chewy chocolate for the handle and divide the rest in half. Divide one half in two again and roll out each piece between sheets of non-stick baking paper until slightly larger than the short ends of the bag. Ease the fondant into folds with a skewer or knitting needle and attach a piece to each end of the cake (it will stick to the buttercream).

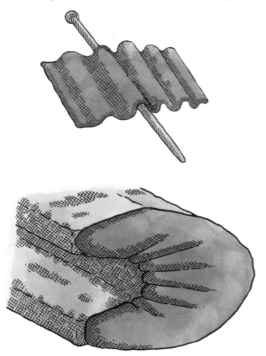

6 Roll the other half of chewy chocolate out between sheets of non-stick baking paper to make a wide strip to cover the whole top of the cake (the side of the bag), approximately 25 cm (10 inches) wide by 30 cm (12 inches) long. Attach it to the cake, from the open side, over the top to the back, and tucking underneath the bottom. Gently press the joins together and wipe away any excess buttercream.

7 To make the inside lining, colour 100 g (4 oz) of the fondant red, leaving it streaky so as to give a 'satin' effect. Roll it out into an oblong 28 cm (11 inches) wide by 7.5 cm (3 inches) long on an icing sugar dusted surface, and lift into the opening of the cake handbag. Press it over the inside base, tucking it well in and easing it to form gentle folds. Trim round the sides but fold any excess at the open end down over the outside of the cake, as it will be covered later by the yellow fondant.

8 Colour approximately 100 g (4 oz) fondant icing golden yellow. Reserve a little for the clasp and fittings and roll the rest into two sausages approximately 46 cm (18 inches) long. Flatten these and attach them round the opening of the cake, securing with some white royal icing applied from a paper icing bag, snipped to make a reasonably sized hole. Make a clasp from a curved wedge of golden fondant (press a knife over it for indentations), and attach to the bag with a little water.

9 Roll out the reserved piece of chewy chocolate between sheets of non-stick baking paper and cut into a strip 46 cm (18 inches) long by 2.5 cm (1 inch) wide. Bend slightly and position on the cake board like a handle. Use the remaining yellow fondant to construct fittings for joining the handle to the bag: form two D-shaped rings from yellow fondant sausages and secure one at each end of the handle where it meets the bag, using a little water. Allow to dry for 1 hour.

10 Add a little water to the gold lustre colour and, with a brush, paint onto the yellow fondant clasp and fittings to enhance their gold colour.

11 Now use your imagination and plasticine-playing abilities to make the objects spilling out of the bag, using the rest of the fondant. Pens and pencils can be constructed with tinted fondant icing placed around wooden skewers; keys can be formed from grey fondant around cocktail sticks. You will have a leftover cake oddment so this could be the basis for a purse or wallet.

To make a sink plug and chain ('everything but the kitchen sink'!), model the plug from black fondant and a fitting for the top in grey fondant. Once in position on the board, pipe a snaking line of royal icing from the top of the plug and stick silver balls to it. Lastly, paint the plug top and keys with silver lustre colour mixed with a little water.

For the crumpled hanky, roll out white fondant into a very thin square and ease into folds – pipe on a pink royal icing monogram if you like. Other items such as lipsticks, bottles of nail varnish, cotton reels and rubbers can be simply moulded from little pieces of coloured fondant icing. Add chocolate coins, boiled sweets or mints to the pile, attaching anything that is loose with a blob of royal icing.

OUT OF THE BLUE

The denim jacket has become a design classic and is a second skin to some. Adorned with badges, patches and pins they are highly personal items, so copy one as closely as you can to get the label and stitching right and everyone will recognize the owner. Reproduce rock band logos for a heavy metal head-banger or motorcycle logos for a hardened biker. The only problem will be how to borrow the precious original garment to study it closely without being found out; you could use motorcycle magazines for reference.

INGREDIENTS

25 cm (10 inch) square shallow sponge cake, using quantity for 23 cm (9 inch) square (p.9)
225 g (8 oz) buttercream (p.17)
apricot glaze (p.17)
1.75 kg (3 lb 14 oz) fondant icing (p.15)
basic paste food colours: blue, black, yellow, brown, and other colours of choice
icing sugar for dusting
liquid food colours: blue, black
225 g (8 oz) royal icing (p.14)
gold and silver lustre powder

OTHER MATERIALS

33 cm (13 inch) square cake board (drum), covered with black sticky-back plastic

SPECIAL EQUIPMENT

bowl
rubber or plastic gloves
small piece of linen or other coarse-textured fabric
paper
absorbent kitchen paper
artist's paint brush
paper piping bags
No. 0 and 1 writing tubes
skewer or knife

NOTE: Allow 3 hours extra preparation time for icing to dry.

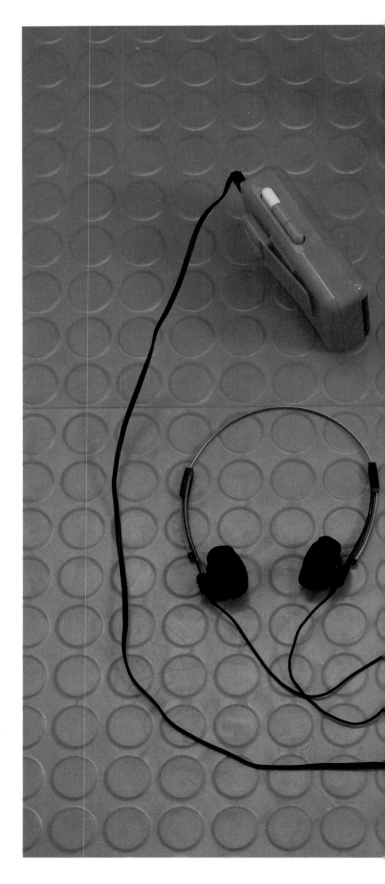

1 Cut the cake in half horizontally, cover the base with buttercream and replace the top; place on the cake board.

2 Soften the outlines of the cake by carving off the corners and rounding the top edge. Brush all over with apricot glaze.

3 Colour 1.5 kg (3 lb 6 oz) of the fondant a light blue with paste colour, adding a little black to tone the colour down. Cover the cake a section of the jacket at a time, rolling the icing out 3 mm (1/8 inch) thick on an icing sugar dusted surface and cutting to the size and shape required. Place the sections loosely on the cake to ensure that the icing falls in natural, crumpled folds.

First apply a round scoop of fondant for the neck, placing to the left of the cake as the jacket is off-centre. Then apply the main panel to the left side of the jacket, which extends to the top of the pocket. Place a central strip down the centre of this panel and then fit in the top section above it, extending to the neckline. Add the pocket flap.

4 Now repeat all these sections for the right side of the jacket, but placing to overlap the left side slightly as in the photograph. Attach a strip around the neck for the collar, and finally cut a long length for the sleeve on the right side. Tuck it in a crumpled fashion from the shoulder down the side, and make a square cuff from fondant to tuck under the base of the jacket.

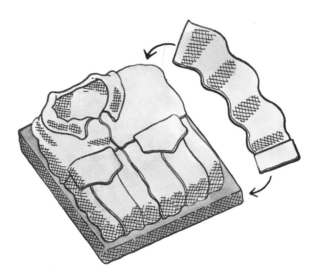

5 Mark the seams on the jacket wherever there is a section join. Press the handle of a knife along the seams to make little 'ridges'. Cut buttonholes into the icing with the point of a knife, down the front of the jacket and on each pocket flap. Leave the icing to dry for 1 hour.

a

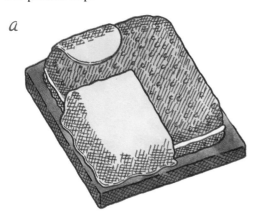

b

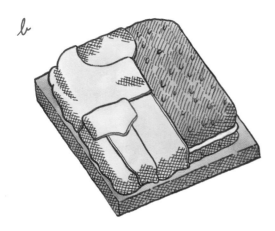

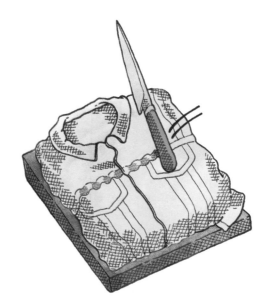

6 Using liquid food colouring, make a blue-black mixture in a bowl and thin it with water. Wearing rubber or plastic gloves, dip a pad of the linen material in the mixture and try the colour out by printing on a spare piece of paper. Adjust the colour if necessary – I found it best to blot the pad on absorbent kitchen paper before printing it onto the cake. In the same way as you would sponge a paint finish, print the linen pad all over the cake to give a denim effect, stippling into difficult areas, such as underneath section joins, with a brush. Leave to dry for at least 2 hours.

7 Colour 50 g (2 oz) of the fondant brown, roll 7 small balls and flatten them to make buttons and, if you like, press a design into them with a skewer or knife. Attach to the cake with a small dot of blue icing and burnish with a little dry gold lustre powder on your finger. Roll out any remaining brown fondant and cut a small rectangle to make the label inside the back collar, attaching it to the cake with a little water on a brush.

8 Colour 30 ml (2 tbsp) of the royal icing dark blue with liquid food colouring and place in a paper piping bag with a No. 1 writing tube. Pipe round the buttonholes in small lines, like stitches. Colour the remaining icing a yellow ochre colour and place in a paper piping bag with a No. 0 writing tube; pipe the stitching with double rows of broken lines on all the seams.

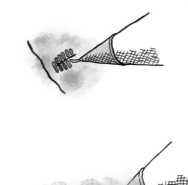

9 Colour small pieces of the remaining fondant bright colours and make different-shaped badges: cut out shapes of fondant icing and either paint appropriately or – for the larger designs – cut out parts of the fondant and insert different-coloured fondant of the same shape in place. Finally, paint the badges with silver lustre mixed with a little water to give a metallic effect.

SEW TASTY

Delicate piping on traditional cakes (which I admire but am not good at) looks very much like lace or embroidery using similar patterns of flowers, ribbons and swags. Take the idea one step further and you have the ideal cake for somebody who is fond of needlework. My best friend Barbara designed this pattern for me in a style called Jacobean work working from an old 1940s leaflet. The ingenuity of the embroiderer was required to fill in the areas with a great variety of stitches, many of which can be copied in coloured icing.

There are plenty of relevant books available, and real embroidery transfers of initials, birds, flowers and many other things form ready-made patterns for pricking onto the top of the cake, so choose your own design to suit the occasion.

INGREDIENTS
20 cm (8 inch) round rich fruit cake (p.7)
apricot glaze (p.17)
500 g (1 lb 2 oz) marzipan (p.15)
500 g (1 lb 2 oz) fondant icing (p.15)
icing sugar for dusting
basic paste food colours: yellow, brown, pink, red, orange, green, or other colours of choice
450 g (1 lb) royal icing (p.14)

OTHER MATERIALS
30 cm (12 inch) round cake board (drum)
large tapestry needle

SPECIAL EQUIPMENT
tracing or greaseproof paper
pencil
pin
paper piping bags
No. 0 and 1 writing tubes

NOTE: Allow at least 1 day extra preparation time for marzipan to dry.

1 Level the top of the cake, turn it over, position it on the cake board, spread with apricot glaze and cover with marzipan (p.21). Leave to dry for at least 24 hours.

2 Reserve approximately 50 g (2 oz) of the fondant icing and colour the remainder a cream colour. Shape the cream fondant icing into a ball then roll out into a circle approximately 38 cm (15 inches) in diameter on an icing sugar dusted surface, trimming if necessary to fit. Carefully lift the fondant circle onto the cake, lightly roll the top to flatten, smooth down the sides for about 2.5 cm (1 inch) and drape the rest in gentle folds around the bottom.

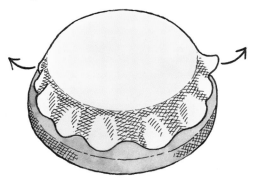

3 Gather up any trimmings of fondant icing, add to the remaining 50 g (2 oz) and colour it all brown – but don't make too much effort to work in the colour as a streaky effect will make it look like wood-grain. Roll out into a long sausage, flatten and trim to make a long strip 70 cm (28 inches) long and 1.5 cm (¾ inch) wide (this can be done in two pieces). Dampen round the sides of the cake, near the top, with a little water on your finger and firmly attach the brown strip as in the picture. Leave for a couple of hours to dry.

4 Trace your chosen design onto tracing or greaseproof paper with a pencil and position it on the top of the cake. With a pin, prick the design through the paper onto the top of the fondant-covered cake.

5 Divide the royal icing, colour and place in separate paper piping bags. I have used seven colours in roughly equal quantities: pink, red, orange, rust, dark brown, moss and dark green. Using a No. 1 writing tube, fill the design with one colour at a time in a variety of stitches as shown here. Use a No. 0 writing tube to do the top cross stitches.

6 Leave one area unfinished and insert a large needle as if the work has been left unfinished. Pipe a thread from the embroidery stitches down the side of the cake and up to the needle, and from the needle again down the side of the cake a little, to give the impression that the needle is threaded.

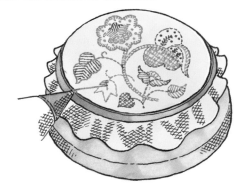

7 Again with a No. 1 writing tube, pipe cross stitches around the bottom of the icing as in the photograph.

8 If you wish to make a decorative skein of wool from spare fondant, cut a cardboard strip and taper it slightly in the middle. Cover with a lump of appropriately coloured fondant, and then pipe lines of 'wool' with coloured royal icing up and down the length. Finally, wrap a strip of yellow fondant round the centre for the label and brush it with gold lustre powder to give a burnished effect.

*i*CED FOLLY

One expression of British eccentricity over the centuries has been the building of follies – brick and concrete structures of all shapes and sizes, towers, pyramids, temples and turrets to name but a few. Apart from the odd hermit or flock of doves, these buildings were largely constructed not for habitation but to satisfy the whim of their creator or to add gothic character to a quiet corner of the garden.

INGREDIENTS

15 cm (6 inch) hexagonal rich fruit cake, using quantity for 15 cm (6 inch) round (p.7)

25 cm (10 inch) hexagonal rich fruit cake, using quantity for 25 cm (10 inch) round (p.7)

liquid food colours: black, brown, green, red

apricot glaze (p.17)

1.25 kg (2 lb 13 oz) marzipan (p.15)

icing sugar for dusting

2.5 kg (5 lb 10 oz) royal icing (p.14)

little fondant icing (p.15)

basic paste colour: black

OTHER MATERIALS

7.5 cm (3 inch) round plaster pillar

20 cm (8 inch) hexagonal cake board (drum)

30 cm (12 inch) hexagonal cake board (drum)

SPECIAL EQUIPMENT

medium artist's paint brush

turntable or upturned plate

fine sandpaper

palette knife

felt-tip pen

tracing or greaseproof paper

non-stick baking paper

nylon piping bag

No. 1 and No. 3 writing tubes

paper piping bags (several)

small jar or matchbox

No. 10 medium star piping tube

NOTE: Allow at least 6½ days extra preparation time for icing to dry.

1 Dilute some black liquid food colour with plenty of water in a cup. With a medium artist's brush, paint the plaster pillar to make it a light grey colour. Leave to dry for a short time.

2 If necessary, trim the cakes level and position them on their respective boards. Brush with apricot glaze and cover with marzipan in sections as you would a square cake (p.22), smoothing the joins at the corners together well. Use 350 g (12 oz) to cover the small cake and the remaining marzipan for the large one. Leave to dry for at least 2 days.

3 Tint 675 g (1 lb 8 oz) of the royal icing a light grey with black liquid food colour. Stand the cakes on a turntable or upturned plate and use half the icing to give both cakes a thin coating (see pages 22–23 on covering a cake with royal icing). Cover the bowl containing the remaining icing with cling film and store in a cool place. Leave the cakes to dry for 24 hours.

4 Trim off any excess icing at the corners of the cakes with a very sharp knife and sand down any lumps and bumps with fine sandpaper. Use the reserved grey royal icing to give both cakes another coat and leave to dry for a further 24 hours.

5 Trim and sand the cakes as before and again stand on upturned plates or a turntable (once the boards are covered with icing they are hard to pick up).

6 Tint 1.35 kg (3 lb) of royal icing a light grey colour as before. Use 450 g (1 lb) of this to give both cakes a final coat and also ice the top and sides of the boards to cover the silver completely, using a palette knife to spread it evenly. Leave to dry for at least 24 hours.

7 Meanwhile, make the run-out decorations: trace the templates shown here with a felt-tip pen onto tracing paper. Measure the sides of the cakes and adjust the length of the upright pieces if necessary. Tape these templates down onto a large board and tape small sheets of non-stick baking paper over them. Place 450 g (1 lb) of grey royal icing in a nylon bag with a No. 1 piping tube and pipe the outlines, and then use paper bags with a medium-sized hole for filling in with the thinner icing (see p.27 on run-outs). Repeat to make seven of each of the upright pieces and fourteen shields (the extras are in case of breakages). Leave all the pieces in a warm dry place for at least 24 hours. Cling film the remaining grey icing and store in a cool place.

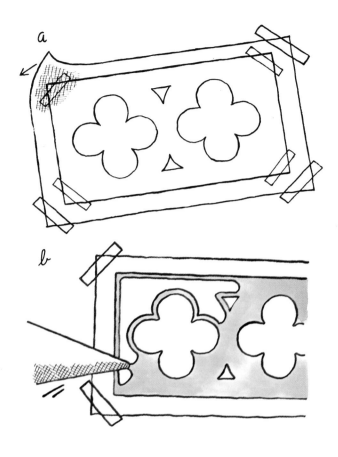

8 Carefully remove the run-out shields from the non-stick paper. Place 30 ml (2 tbsp) of the reserved grey icing in a paper piping bag, snip a medium-sized hole in the end and roughly pipe a blob of icing on the back of each shield. Press one shield into the centre of each side of both cakes.

9 Carefully remove the other run-outs from the non-stick paper. Place a No. 3 writing tube in a paper piping bag and fill it with 60–75 ml (4–5 tbsp) of the remaining royal icing. Pipe along the top edge of one cake and press a run-out piece into position. Support it against a small jar or matchbox placed on the top of the cake. Pipe down one side of this run-out piece and along the next side of the cake and press another piece in, pushing it right up to the first piece which will stick to it and no longer need supporting. Continue like this around both the cakes.

10 Place a little icing in two more paper piping bags. Snip a small hole in one and cut the other to a point. Pipe flower designs onto the shields using the plain bag for lines and dots, and the other for leaves and petals (see p.25 on piping with a paper piping bag).

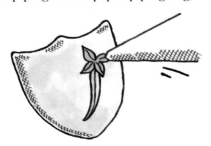

11 Place the remaining grey icing in a nylon piping bag with a medium No. 10 star piping tube and pipe lines around all the joins and edges on the cakes, along the top and bottom of the run-out pieces, down each corner and where the cakes join the boards. Stick the grey plaster pillar in the centre of the small cake with a blob of icing and leave to dry for 12 hours.

12 Place the small cake and its board inside the top of the large cake. Make 450 g (1 lb) of royal icing. Colour a third of this dark brown. Divide this brown icing between two paper piping bags and cut a large hole in one and a smaller hole in the other. Pipe the trunk and large branches of the vine up one side of the cake with the large-holed bag and smaller branches and roots with the other. This is an opportunity to cover up any mistakes and cracks in the grey icing so choose the best side of the cake to leave clear and the worst side to cover with the vine!

13 Colour half the remaining royal icing green and half russet-red. Use two-thirds of the green in paper piping bags (you may need more than one), cut at an angle as before (see step 10) to pipe green leaves all over one side of the vine.

14 Place green icing down one side and red down the other of another paper piping bag. Cut the end at an angle as before and pipe variegated leaves down the middle of the vine. Continue piping leaves with a bag filled with red icing to finish off the vine.

15 Colour a little fondant icing a light grey with paste colour and model a figure, animal or other symbol to top off the central pillar (mine represents the 'hare' to the family estate!).

tHE ONE THAT GOT AWAY

The lone fisherman can always boast of the leviathan that tugged the line, made a meal of the bait and escaped to fight another day. This cake represents that fish, a smile on its lips and a twinkle in its eye, for we all know that this rare giant breed exists only in the sea of the imagination.

The marbled effect made by rolling different shades of fondant together is evocative of water, and lustre powder colours give a silvery look to the fish scales.

INGREDIENTS

23 cm (9 inch) square rich fruit cake (p.7)
icing sugar for dusting
1 kg (2 lb 4 oz) marzipan (p.15)
apricot glaze (p.17)
1 kg (2 lb 4 oz) fondant icing (p.15)
basic paste food colours: blue, black, green, yellow, pink
green lustre powder
silver lustre powder

OTHER MATERIALS

21 × 60 cm (8½ × 24 inch) plank of wood, approx. 1 cm (½ inch thick), covered with wood-grain sticky-back plastic
cocktail stick

SPECIAL EQUIPMENT

greaseproof paper
pen top
scraps of thin card
spice jars
non-stick baking paper
fine artist's paint brush

NOTE: Allow at least 1 day extra preparation time for marzipan to dry.

1 Cut the cake in half vertically and place the pieces end to end. Following the diagram, draw and cut out a fish-shaped template from greaseproof paper. Lay this on the cake and cut out the fish shape. Use an offcut of cake to extend the tail end and carve the whole thing so it is rounded on top, cutting away underneath to make it more realistic.

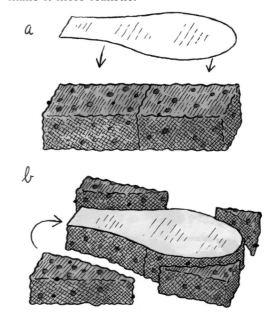

2 On an icing sugar dusted surface, roll out 75 g (3 oz) of the marzipan to an 11.5 × 7.5 cm (4½ × 3 inch) oblong and use to sandwich together the two larger cake pieces: brush the ends of both pieces with apricot glaze, place the marzipan between and press together. Position the cake on the wood board, towards one end to allow room for the tail.

3 Repeat the previous step with 50 g (2 oz) of marzipan to join on the tail piece, but use a cocktail stick give extra support.

4 Use 75 g (3 oz) of marzipan to patch up any uneven parts and joins and brush the fish's belly with apricot glaze. Attach a thickly rolled piece of 150 g (5½ oz) marzipan to build up the top of the belly, blending it into a general rounded shape. Brush the whole cake with apricot glaze, not forgetting underneath the bottom edges.

5 Covering the cake with one whole piece of marzipan makes a better finished surface. Roll out the remaining marzipan on a large icing sugar dusted surface to the approximate shape of the cake fish, remembering to make it large enough so that it can be tucked under. Carefully lift it onto the cake (support it with a rolling pin) and smooth down all over with your hands, tucking the edges under and trimming off any excess. Leave to dry for at least 24 hours.

6 Colour 650 g (1 lb 7 oz) of the fondant blue-grey. Use 50 g (2 oz) of this to build the shape up around the gill, eye and mouth (see diagram). On an icing sugar dusted surface, roll out another 500 g (1 lb 2 oz) of the blue-grey fondant to an area large enough to virtually cover the cake. Lay this over the fish, including the head but avoiding the very top edge; smooth down and tuck under with your hands.

7 Trim the blue-grey fondant in a straight line down the whole length of the fish, about two-thirds up its body (the lateral line), and remove any fondant above this line. Press the blue-grey fondant into the facial features, sharpening the line of the gills with the back of a knife. Trim away any excess fondant around the wood board and collect up the trimmings and add to the rest of the blue-grey fondant.

8 Reserving 25 g (1 oz) for the eye and plaque, divide the remaining white fondant in two; colour one piece a light grey-blue and the other light green. Remember that badly kneaded-in colours can look quite effective. Take small blobs of each of these colours and some of the darker blue-grey fondant trimmings, and line them up on an icing sugar dusted surface, alternating the colours. Press all the pieces together then roll out flat to give a stripy marbled effect. Roll out to a length to cover the top side of the fish. Trim the bottom edge straight and lay on the fish cake so that it butts up neatly to the blue-grey fondant. Smooth the join together and tuck the edges under at the top. Cut away any excess and reserve.

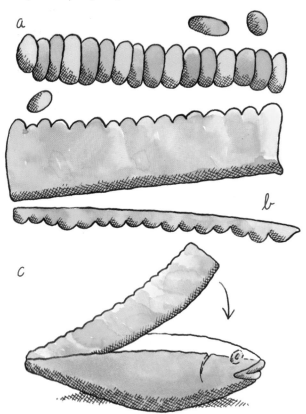

9 Press a pen top into the fondant all over to give the effect of scales.

10 Use spare pieces of fondant, build out the basis of the tail and a support for the two larger fins on the body – attach two fondant lumps to the top and bottom sides where the fins will go. With folded cardboard or spice jars and anything that comes to hand, build up supports on the wood board where the two fins and the tail will go. Top each support with a flat piece of cardboard covered with non-stick baking paper.

11 Gather up all the offcuts of fondant and add some black colour to parts of it to darken the colour. Roll it all together again to give a dark marbled effect. Roll out on an icing sugar dusted surface and cut out all the fins and the tail, marking lines down the surface with the back of a knife before attaching them to the cake with a little water. Leave to dry for at least 1 hour before carefully removing the supports underneath the larger fins.

12 Colour a small pea-sized piece of the reserved fondant yellow and press into the eye socket. Mix green lustre powder with a little water and with a fine artist's brush paint the occasional scale on the body. Add a little green paste colour to strengthen the hue and paint a few more; also paint the lateral line along the length of the fish. Silver the fins and tail with a little lustre powder on your finger.

13 With a brush and a little flesh-pink paste colour thinned with water, tint the mouth and around the eye and gills. With a little black paste, fill in the pupil of the eye.

14 If liked, colour the remaining scrap of white fondant light grey, roll out and cut out a small oblong shape to resemble a plaque. Press a date or name into it with the point of a knife or skewer and allow to dry for a short time. Position on the wood board and paint with silver lustre powder mixed with a little water.

SOCKS & TIE AGAIN

In his poem 'Christmas' John Betjeman wrote of 'Loving fingers tying strings, Around those tissued fripperies, The sweet and silly Christmas things, Bath salts and inexpensive scent, And hideous tie so kindly meant'. There are people who have a drawerful of such gifts received every birthday and Christmas, some of them bought in a hurry at shops that specialize in selling just knickers, socks or ties. But what do you give someone who apparently has everything they need? A cake of one of these ubiquitous but 'kindly meant' gifts is the ideal antidote to birthday boredom. The ingredients given here are enough to make one 'gift' cake.

INGREDIENTS

15 cm (6 inch) round or 13 cm (5 inch) square rich fruit cake (p.7)
apricot glaze (p.17)
300 g (11 oz) marzipan (p.15)
icing sugar for dusting
500 g (1 lb 2 oz) fondant icing (p.15)
basic paste food colours: red, blue, black or green

OTHER MATERIALS

15 cm (6 inch) round or 13 cm (5 inch) square cake board

SPECIAL EQUIPMENT

non-stick baking paper
small heart-shaped or round cutter, or a piping tube

NOTE: Allow at least 1 day extra preparation time for marzipan to dry.

1 Trim the cake level and position it on the cake board, securing with a little apricot glaze if necessary. Place the board on a piece of non-stick baking paper and cover the cake with marzipan (p.21) so that the board is completely hidden. Leave to dry for at least 24 hours.

2 Colour 200 g (7 oz) of the fondant the main colour and 200 g (7 oz) the second colour. Measure the depth and circumference of the cake, add 5 mm (¼ inch) to the depth measurement and roll out a strip this size from the main colour, on an icing sugar dusted surface. Attach it around the side of the cake (with a little water to secure if necessary) so that the top stands above the cake.

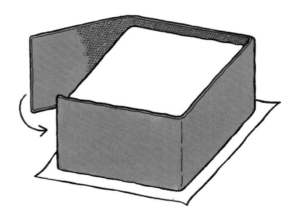

3 With a small cutter or piping tube, cut out shapes randomly around the sides of the cake and pull out the pieces of fondant with the point of a knife. Roll out half the second colour fondant, cut out the same shapes and insert them into the holes in the sides of the cake, smoothing the joins together.

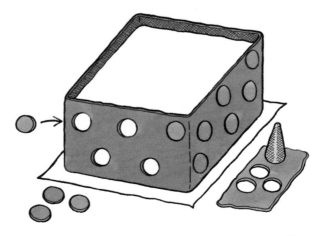

4 Cut out strips of thinly rolled fondant in the second colour and stick just inside the top edges of the cake, gently crumpled to resemble tissue paper.

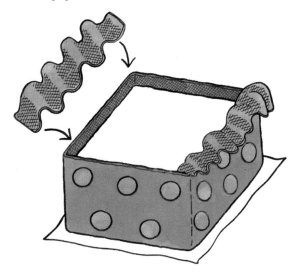

5 Colour the remaining fondant, grey for socks or two colours such as blue and green for a tie. Roll out: either cut out two sock shapes and score on lines and details with the back of a knife, or for a tie, roll the two colours out, cut into thin strips and butt the alternate colour strips together. Roll lightly with a rolling pin to join the strips together and carefully cut out a tie shape.

6 Carefully lift the 'present' onto the top of the cake and attach with a little water. Position more 'tissue' strips of the second colour around to make it look as if the present is emerging from the tissue wrapping. Leave it to dry for 2–3 hours.

7 Remove the cake from the non-stick baking paper and serve, either on another board or tray or directly on the table as shown in the photograph.

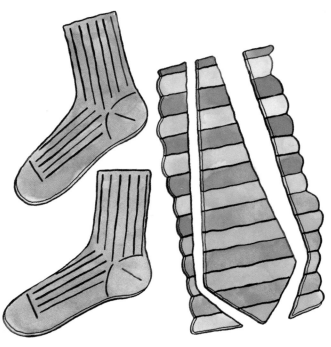

CANDY MAN

It was cheering to find that all the sweets I remember from my childhood, pink shrimps, flying saucers, milk bottles and love hearts, are still available – plus many more wonderful shapes and flavours. I spent at least fifteen minutes at the children's pick-and-mix, carefully sorting out the colours I wanted with my scoop, much to the amusement of my small fellow pickers. Adults seem to find these sweets as irresistible as children do: at the studio we had to stop ourselves eating them so that we would have enough left for the photograph, and the actual cake was swiftly consumed later. Use your ingenuity and different shapes and shades (there are surprisingly few suitable ones for face colours!) of sweets to create your candy portrait, even placing them on top of each other to follow the contours of the face.

INGREDIENTS
two 23 × 33 cm (9 × 13 inch) Swiss roll sponges (p.14)

750 g (1 lb 10 oz) buttercream (p.17)

liquid food colours: pink, yellow

at least 750 g (1 lb 10 oz) mixed multi-coloured sweets, including liquorice shoelaces

OTHER MATERIALS
30 × 25 cm (12 × 10 inch) cake board, cut from a 30 cm (12 inch) square and then covered with green sticky-back plastic

SPECIAL EQUIPMENT
small palette knife

1 Colour a quarter of the buttercream pink and the rest yellow.

2 Trim the ends of the cakes so that they are both 28 cm (11 inches) long. Position one cake centrally on the cake board, spread it with approximately a third of the yellow buttercream and place the other cake on top.

3 Reserving a little for sticking the sweets together, spread the pink buttercream over the top of the cake in a rough head and shoulders shape, using a small palette knife. Cover the sides and the rest of the top of the cake with the remaining yellow buttercream.

4 Sort the sweets out into colours. Start by choosing sweets for the nose, mouth and eyes and position these on the cake by pressing them into the buttercream a little and using the leftover pink buttercream to stick any sweets that are piled up on top of each other. Choose suitable sweets for the cheeks and lips and put brown or black sweets where the beard will go.

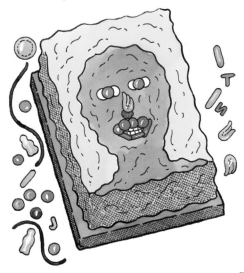

5 Use green, orange and yellow sweets for the background, mauve and purple for the body, and all the leftover colours to cover the sides of the cake. Lastly roll up liquorice shoelaces to make the beard and fold and snip some small pieces to make the hair and the eyebrow line.

CALAVERA

On November 2nd, All Souls Day, the people of Mexico honour the deceased in their Day of The Dead celebrations. Unlike our Hallowe'en of ghoulies, ghosties and goblins, this day is a party of joyful remembrance. Cemeteries are cleaned up and individual graves are brightly painted and decorated with flowers and candles. Clay and papier maché skulls and dressed skeletons made by local artists can be bought at markets to decorate the house. Children play with skeleton toys and eat colourful sugar skulls; special food and bread is cooked and a festive atmosphere prevails.

This is my rendition of, and tribute to, that folk art. Make it for Hallowe'en or a weird friend.

Light fruit cake made with multi-coloured glacé cherries echoes the external decoration and I used a plastic joke-shop skull as a model to carve the right shape.

INGREDIENTS

two 15 cm (6 inch) round light fruit cakes (p.8)
icing sugar for dusting
750 g (1 lb 10 oz) marzipan (p.15)
apricot glaze (p.17)
500 g (1 lb 2 oz) fondant icing (p.15)
225 g (8 oz) royal icing (p.14)
basic paste food colours: yellow, blue, and bright colours of choice

OTHER MATERIALS

20 cm (8 inch) round cake board (drum), covered with gold cake board paper

SPECIAL EQUIPMENT

small cutters (optional)
fine artist's paint brush
paper piping bags

NOTE: Allow at least 1 day extra preparation time for marzipan to dry.

1 If necessary trim the tops of the cakes a little to level them. On an icing sugar dusted surface, roll out 200 g (7 oz) of the marzipan to a circle roughly the size of the top of a cake. Brush the top of one cake with apricot glaze, lay the circle of marzipan on top, brush the bottom of the other cake with glaze and position over the marzipan, slightly off centre (see diagram). Turn the whole cake on its side and trim a little off the back of the bottom cake so that it leans back when set the right way up again.

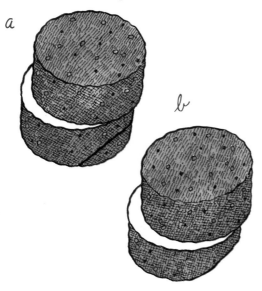

2 Cut a slice off each side of the cake and attach the pieces to the top of the cake to heighten it, using a disc of 50 g (2 oz) marzipan and apricot glaze to sandwich the pieces of cake together.

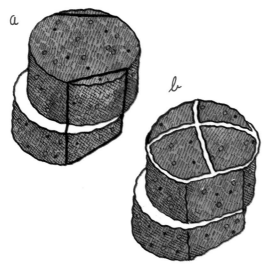

3 Carve the cake roughly to shape, cutting away under the cheekbones and into the eyesockets and nose. Carve the top and back of the skull as smooth as possible and use 150 g (5½ oz) marzipan to build up the outside of the eye sockets and generally patch up any unwanted holes and round off any flat areas like the sides of the skull. Place the cake on the cake board and brush with apricot glaze.

4 Roll out the remaining marzipan on an icing sugar dusted surface to a circle large enough to entirely cover the cake. Lay the marzipan over the cake, smoothing it down all round and easing it into all the features. It may not stretch right into the eye sockets so let it tear as you push it in and patch up with an offcut. Trim off any excess marzipan and work together any joins with the flat blade of a knife. The smoother the marzipan is now, the better the surface of the finished cake will be. Neaten the bottom edge and leave the cake to dry for at least 24 hours.

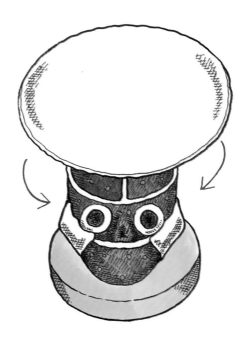

5 Colour 350 g (12 oz) of the fondant icing cream and use approximately 50 g (2 oz) of it to build up raised areas for the nose and teeth (see diagram). Then roll out the remainder on an icing sugar dusted surface to a circle large enough to completely cover the skull. Supporting it on the rolling pin, lift the fondant onto the cake and smooth down all round. Cut off any folds of icing and work the resulting joins together with your fingers. Ease the fondant into the eyesockets and nose (it is more pliable than marzipan but if it does tear, patch the hole and cover it with decoration later) and press lines into the teeth with the back of a pointed knife to indent rather than cut the icing. Neaten the bottom edge, tucking under excess fondant.

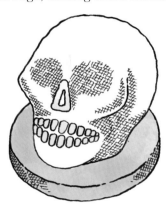

6 Colour 100 g (4 oz) fondant various bright colours and, mould into decorative shapes such as flower petals and spirals, or roll out on an icing sugar dusted surface and cut out shapes with a knife or cutters. Apply to the cake with a dampened brush.

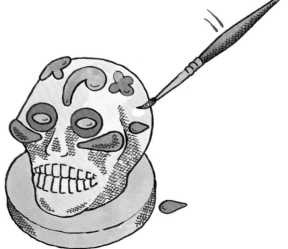

7 Divide the royal icing and shade in various bright colours, 15–30 ml (1–2 tbsp) at a time. Place each quantity in a small paper piping bag and snip a small hole in the end. Pipe dots and squiggles in various colours over the cake until it is completely covered.

8 Colour the remaining fondant blue, roll out thinly on an icing sugar dusted surface and cut pieces to fit the cake board around the skull. Position these pieces on the drum, butting them up to the cake, smoothing together the joins and trimming neatly round the edge.

PERSONAL SERVICES

What does that grey-suited man sitting opposite you on the train wear while relaxing in the evening?

Those in a sober profession – manager, lawyer, accountant, politician – should find this satirical impression of their private lifestyle highly amusing. There are, of course, some who will not, so choose the subject of this cake with care – it may offend or even be too close to the truth for comfort!

A poseable teenage doll is a useful model to get the proportions of the figure right, or ask someone to pose for you. A cake armchair makes a good base for modelling figures on.

INGREDIENTS

18 cm (7 inch) square rich fruit cake (p.7)
18 cm (7 inch) square shallow rich fruit cake. using quantity for 15 cm (6 inch) square (p.7)
apricot glaze (p.17)
1 kg (2 lb 4 oz) marzipan (p.15)
icing sugar for dusting
750 g (1 lb 10 oz) fondant icing (p.15)
basic paste food colours: green, black, pink, red
225 g (8 oz) royal icing (p.14)
opaque white food colour (optional)
silver lustre powder

OTHER MATERIALS

25 cm (10 inch) square cake board (drum)
cocktail stick
wooden skewer

SPECIAL EQUIPMENT

spice jar
non-stick baking paper
paper piping bags
cocktail stick or skewer
No. 1 writing tube
fine artist's paint brush

NOTE: Allow at least 1 day extra preparation time for marzipan to dry.

1 Trim the top of the deeper cake to level it, cut a 6 cm (2½ inch) strip off one side and reserve to make the figure; the rest will form the seat of the armchair.

2 Cut a quarter off one side of the shallower cake and cut this piece in half, rounding the corners of one end of each piece to make the arms of the chair. Round off two corners of the main part of the cake to make the back.

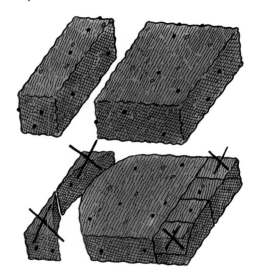

3 Assemble the chair pieces towards the back of the cake board, sticking them together with glaze and filling any gaps with marzipan.

4 Spread the whole chair with apricot glaze and cover with marzipan, following the same principles for covering a square cake (p.22); roll out 800 g (1 lb 12 oz) of the marzipan fairly thin on an icing sugar dusted surface. Cut two long pieces to fit over the sides and arms, a long wide piece to wrap over the front and seat and finally a piece for the whole back chair, stretching from the seat up, over and down the back of the chair. Attach the marzipan pieces to the cake, filling any gaps such as over the arms.

5 Cut one end off the remaining slab of cake for the legs of the figure. Carve the larger piece of slab roughly into the shape of a torso, cutting a sloping line up to the shoulders and rounding the belly. Carve the other piece into the shape of crossed-over thighs down to the knee. Attach both pieces to the chair with apricot glaze and brush all over with glaze. Roll out the remaining marzipan and lay it over the figure, easing it carefully into the carved shape and smoothing down with your hands. Leave to dry for at least 24 hours.

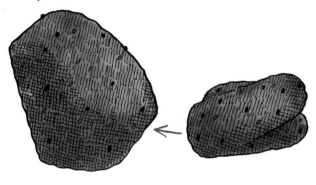

6 Colour 500 g (1 lb 2 oz) of the fondant icing pale green, roll out 350 g (12 oz) of it on an icing sugar dusted surface and cover the chair in a similar way to the marzipan, fitting it round the body. Dampening the marzipan with a little water will help the fondant stick more firmly if there is any problem.

7 Using 100 g (4 oz) of the green fondant, roll out thin strips approximately 1.5 cm (¾ inch) wide and attach around the bottom of the chair with a little water, pleating the strips to give the effect of a frill. Colour the remaining 50 g (2 oz) and any trimmings of fondant a slightly darker shade of green and keep tightly wrapped to make the cushions later.

8 Reserve a small piece of the remaining fondant icing and colour the rest flesh-pink. Stick a cocktail stick half way into the top of the torso, thread a small ball of fondant onto this to make the neck and another ball on top of this for the head (smaller than the finished size).

9 Cut a wooden skewer down to size, mould one lower leg and foot from flesh-pink fondant around it and press into position in front of the chair. Model a similar foot and leg around a cut-down wooden skewer, up to the knee with a bit extra to attach it, and leave to one side to dry for a short time.

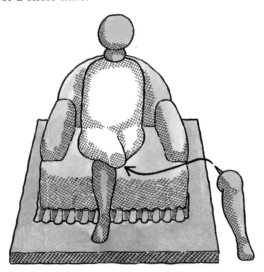

10 Model both arms and hands and attach to the sides of the body. Stick the raised leg in position with a little water and work the fondant into the marzipan. Put something small (like a spice jar covered with a piece of non-stick baking paper) under the foot to support it while it dries.

11 Build up any features on the torso such as the pectoral muscles with little bits of fondant, then roll out a large oblong piece of flesh-pink fondant and lay over the remaining bare areas of the figure: the thighs, torso, shoulders and a little down the back. Work all the joins together and smooth the figure all over, accentuating the crossed-over legs by indenting the back of a knife into the join.

12 The face is made like a full head mask, so make a circle of fondant large enough to cover the whole head, pull out a nose and chin and place over the head. Model into shape, pressing to neaten the back of the head and the neck. Indent the mouth with a cocktail stick, make eye sockets with a skewer, make two ears from fondant and attach them to the head with a little water, and insert two tiny balls of white fondant into the eye sockets. Leave to dry for a couple of hours.

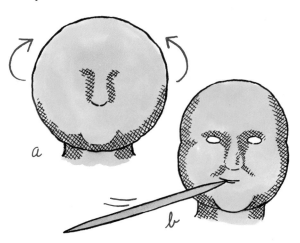

13 Colour the remaining fondant black and dress the figure up with little strips of black 'leather' – follow the photograph if you like, and attach the pieces with a little water. Make two small cushions from the reserved dark green fondant and tuck these in under the arms. (These will help to hide any untidy joins there.)

14 Put 15 ml (1 tbsp) of white royal icing in a paper piping bag, snip the end to make a small hole and pipe on the moustache and hair; similarly pipe the chains and studs with 15 ml (1 tbsp) of grey-coloured royal icing.

15 Using a fine brush and black paste food colour, paint on the fishnet stockings, facial features, chest and arm hair and tint the moustache and hair a little to give a greying effect. If you have white food colour, paint a few white hairs onto the chest. Using silver lustre colour mixed with a little water, paint the studs and chains a metallic silver.

16 Colour 15 ml (1 tbsp) of royal icing brick-red and reserve. Colour the rest green, and put 15 ml (1 tbsp) of it in a piping bag with a No. 1 writing tube. Thin the rest with a little water and put into another paper piping bag with a large opening (see run-outs on p.27). With the thicker icing, pipe the outline and fringe of a rug on the cake board and then fill in with the thinner icing, allowing it to run into the whole area. Use a cocktail stick to encourage the icing into any awkward holes, and to prick out any air bubbles. Allow to dry for 30 minutes.

17 Finally, put the brick-red icing into a paper icing bag, snip the end to make a small hole and pipe patterns onto the rug.

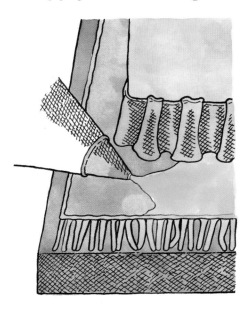

87

rIGHT ON CUE

*Cakes have been made of most sports –
football and cricket pitches, tennis courts and
snooker tables to name but a few. While this
is a special (and surprising) cake for a pool
player, it is also a hint on how to tackle other
sports in a different way, concentrating more
on the equipment and clothes in life-size
representations and less on those great
expanses of green.
If you wish to personalize this cake further,
replace the numbers with letters to spell out a
message and hide chocolates under the hollow
balls for an extra surprise.*

INGREDIENTS

25 × 20 cm (10 × 8 inch) chocolate sponge cake, using quantity for 18 cm (7 inch) square (p.9)
1 kg (2 lb 4 oz) fondant icing (p.15)
basic paste food colours: yellow, blue, red, violet, orange, green, black, brown
icing sugar for dusting
300 g (11 oz) chocolate buttercream (p.17)
15 chocolates (optional)

OTHER MATERIALS

34 cm (13½ inch) equilateral triangle cake board, cut from a 34 cm (13½ inch) square and covered with green sticky-back plastic

SPECIAL EQUIPMENT

8–15 size 3 eggs, in egg boxes
small piece of bread or plasticine
1.5 cm (¾ inch) round cutter or bottle top
pencil
small sheet of paper
fine artist's paint brush
butter or palette knife
ruler

NOTE: Allow at least 12 hours extra preparation time
for fondant to dry.

1 Colour the fondant icing in the following quantities, keeping each piece well wrapped in cling film until needed: 40 g (1½ oz) each of yellow, dark blue, red, violet, orange, dark green, maroon and black; 350 g (12 oz) cream and the remaining fondant brown (don't work this colour in too well, to ensure a good, wood-grain effect when rolled out).

2 Roll the yellow piece of fondant into a ball then flatten with a rolling pin on a surface well dusted with icing sugar to make a circle approximately 9 cm (3½ inches) in diameter. Dust the wide end of one egg with icing sugar and lay the fondant circle over it; smooth it down carefully over the egg with the palm of your hand. Press a lump of bread or plasticine into the bottom of one of the holes in an egg box and stand the covered egg in it so that the fondant doesn't touch the side of the box. Repeat with the other seven colours the remaining seven eggs.

3 Roll out 50 g (2 oz) of the cream fondant to the same thickness as you have rolled the coloured fondant and cut out eight circles with a cutter or bottle top. Use the same cutter to cut circles right through the fondant on the top of the eggs. Pull out the coloured icing and insert a cream circle on each egg. Smooth the joins.

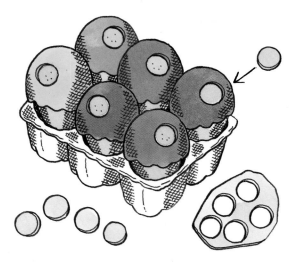

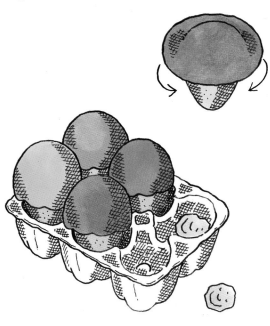

4 Make seven plain cream balls in the same way as the coloured balls, using 40 g (1½ oz) fondant at a time. Leave all the eggs to dry for 12 hours or overnight. If you haven't got 15 eggs spare, make the balls in two separate batches, ensuring the eggs are clean and dry before making the second batch.

5 When the fondant is dry, trim neatly round the edge with a sharp knife and remove any excess; gently ease the fondant off the eggs and stand the hemispheres on plates. With a pencil, gently draw round the cutter used before on top of the cream balls to mark the circles. Using the straight edge of a piece of paper as a guide, pencil the stripes onto the cream balls.

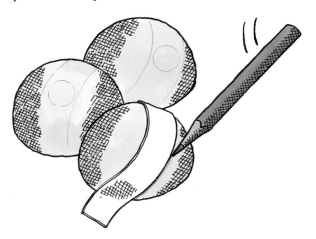

6 With a fine brush, paint the numbers on the cream circles in the coloured balls to match their colours and paint the stripes and numbers on the cream balls. You may wish to put an age or date on the balls for a birthday but here are the numbers on a real set: coloured balls with cream dots – yellow 1, blue 2, red 3, violet 4, orange 5, green 6, maroon 7, black 8; striped balls – yellow 9, blue 10, red 11, violet 12, orange 13, green 14, maroon 15. Most of these colours can be used straight from their tubs but be sure to rinse the brush thoroughly between each colour. If it is necessary to mix shades, use a white plate as a palette and remove the paste colour from its tub with a cocktail stick (see pages 23–4 for painting tips).

7 Trim the cake level, cut up as shown in the diagram and position on the cake board, sticking the pieces together with a little chocolate buttercream. Spread the rest of the buttercream over the top of the cake and a little down the sides with a butter or palette knife. Press the fondant balls into the buttercream, butting them up to each other. A chocolate can be hidden under each ball if liked.

8 On an icing sugar dusted surface, roll out the reserved brown fondant into a sausage approximately 33 cm (13 inches) long. Roll it flat with a rolling pin to make a strip 9 cm (3½ inches) wide. Cutting against a ruler, slice into three long straight-edged strips each 3 cm (1¼ inch) wide. Position these around the edge of the cake, pressing them lightly against the sides and trimming the ends to butt together tidily.

a

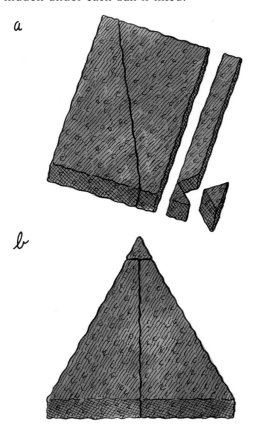

b

SHINING PYRAMID

Every pulp novel adventurer has a goal (besides discovering lost worlds of course) – gold, jewels, or some antique religious or even magical artefact. Help someone keep up with the Indiana Joneses by making them this mysterious glowing treasure apparently plundered from an ancient tomb.

INGREDIENTS

18 cm (7 inch) square rich fruit cake (p.7)
13 cm (5 inch) square rich fruit cake (p.7)
apricot glaze (p.17)
700 g (1 lb 9 oz) marzipan (p.15)
icing sugar for dusting
800 g (1 lb 12 oz) fondant icing (p.15)
basic paste food colours: yellow, brown, and other colours of choice
gold balls
opaque white food colouring

OTHER MATERIALS

20 cm (8 inch) square cake board (drum), covered with gold cake board paper
15 cm (6 inch) square cake board, covered with gold cake board paper
4 small brass doorknobs
foil or gold paper (optional)
a small torch, marbles, beads or other precious looking items (optional)

SPECIAL EQUIPMENT

bradawl or pointed tool
pencil
ruler
tracing or greaseproof paper
thick paper or thin card
scissors
flat skewer, spoon or other flat modelling tools
fine artist's paint brush

NOTE: Allow at least 1 day extra preparation time for marzipan to dry.

1 If necessary, trim the top of the 18 cm (7 inch) square cake to level it and place upside down on the 20 cm (8 inch) square cake board. If you wish to put a torch or some treasure in the centre of the cake, cut a hole in the top large enough to hold it and line with extra marzipan attached with apricot glaze. Brush the cake all over with apricot glaze and cover with 500 g (1 lb 2 oz) of the marzipan in the usual way (p.22)

2 With a bradawl or similar pointed tool, make a hole approximately 2.5 cm (1 inch) in from each corner of the 15 cm (6 inch) square cake board and screw the brass doorknobs through the board so that the knobs are underneath and the screws come up through the top.

3 Using a pencil and ruler, trace the two triangular shapes shown below onto tracing or greaseproof paper, transfer onto thick paper or thin card and cut out with scissors to make two templates.

4 Hold template 1 against one side of the 13 cm (5 inch) square cake and cut away the cake all the way through on either side of the card. Hold template 2 against one sloping side of the cake and cut away the cake either side in the same way – you now have a flat-topped pyramid of cake. Position it on the 15 cm (6 inch) cake board, pressing onto the protruding screws of the doorknobs. Brush with glaze.

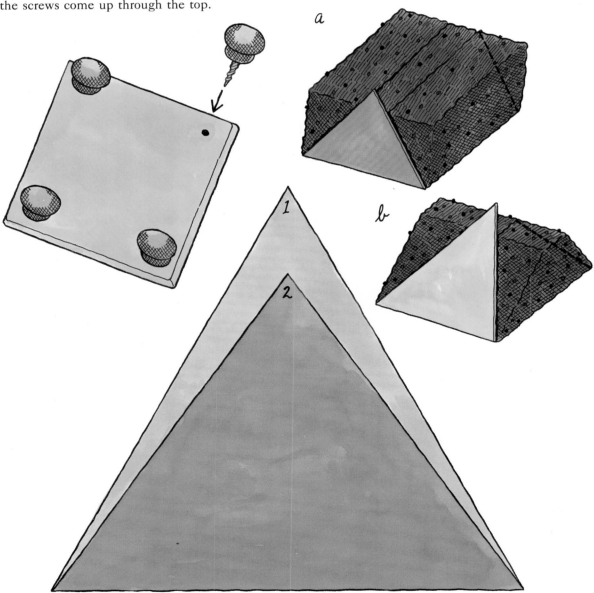

5 Roll out the remaining marzipan on an icing sugar dusted surface and, using template 2 as a guide, cut out four triangles of marzipan and attach them to the cake, smoothing together the joins. Fold down the points at the top because you can build up a perfect point for the pyramid later with fondant. Leave both cakes to dry for at least 24 hours.

6 Colour all the fondant icing 'golden sand', using yellow and a little brown food colouring. Roll out 550 g (1 lb 3 oz) of it on an icing sugar dusted surface to a 33 cm (13 inch) square. Lift this over the square cake, roll the top lightly and then smooth down the sides with your hands. Cut away any excess fondant, smooth together any resulting joins and tidy around the bottom of the board. If you have cut a hole in the middle of the cake, cut the fondant and fold down neatly into the hole.

7 Gather together any fondant offcuts and use a little to make up the point of the pyramid. Add the rest to the remaining golden fondant. Dampen the pyramid cake with a little water on your fingers. Roll out the remaining fondant on an icing sugar dusted board to a long curved strip, approximately 25 × 18 cm (10 × 7 inches). Wrap this around the pyramid cake, smoothing down all round over the corners, trimming off any excess and smoothing together any resulting joins. Neaten the bottom edge as before and press edible gold balls up the corner edges of both cakes.

8 Plan your design on paper then copy it freehand onto the cakes, pressing lightly at first and then more heavily when you are sure of the design. Use implements such as a straight meat skewer or the ends of spoons or forks to emboss the design. Press the edge of a ruler into the cake for the long straight lines and use the end of a pen to make the circles. Leave to dry.

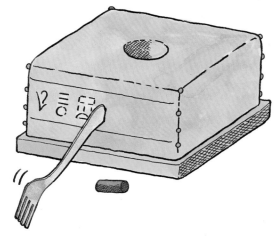

9 With a fine artist's paint brush, paint into the embossed designs, mixing the red, blue and green paste colours with opaque white colour to give strong opaque shades that will be unaffected by the sandy colour of the icing.

10 If you have left a hole in the square cake for some treasure, line it with foil or gold paper left over from covering the cake boards to protect the cake and make it look tidy; you can then fill with your chosen surprise. Place the pyramid cake centrally on the square cake.

rATHER MOORE-ISH

After having consumed a miniature Henry Moore such as this you will find yourself fantasizing what flavour a real modern sculpture might be – what quantity of sugar, flour and eggs would it take to make a massive reclining figure and how many people would it feed? Hard materials such as bronze or stone are a complete contrast to soft buttercream and sponge cake but the gentle lines and curves translate well to this edible medium.

Carve the cake until you are happy with the shape but don't bother to make it too smooth as squarish corners can be rounded with the buttercream. The buttercream darkens when it is melted with a hot knife so do not make the original shade too dark. It is also possible to go over the whole cake quickly with a hot hair dryer to obtain a shiny finish.

INGREDIENTS
23 cm (9 inch) square sponge cake (p.9)

apricot glaze (p.17)

450 g (1 lb) buttercream (p.17)

basic paste food colours: brown

OTHER MATERIALS
35 × 20 cm (14 × 8 inch) cake board (drum), cut from a 35 cm (14 inch) square and then covered with brown or wood-effect sticky-back plastic

cocktail stick

SPECIAL EQUIPMENT
small palette or flat knife

paper piping bag

1 Cut the cake roughly into quarters. Level the top of two of the pieces and place the other two pieces on top of them, not necessarily squarely.

2 Start carving! Take the pieces of cake apart to cut the holes and carve the head from an offcut, securing it on with a cocktail stick.

3 When you are happy with the shape, stick the pieces together with apricot glaze, position on the cake board and brush all over with apricot glaze.

4 Colour the buttercream a light browny-bronze colour, reserve 15 ml (1 tbsp) of it and roughly cover the cake with the rest, making sure to get it right into the holes. Smooth over the surface with a small palette knife.

5 Colour the reserved buttercream a darker shade of brown and fill the piping bag with it. Snip a small hole in the end and pipe small dots of buttercream over a few areas of the sculpture, working them in with the point of a knife to give subtle colour variation.

6 Heat a small palette knife in boiling water, wipe dry and smooth the surface of the cake, reheating as the knife cools. This will melt and darken the buttercream a little, giving the cake a sculptural appearance.

SWEET MEMORIES

There can be nothing more embarrassing for a nervous teenager trying to impress a special friend than having the baby pictures paraded out by mum. It can be very nostalgic too – I have made a similar cake for a golden anniversary with a wedding photograph and a suitable message on the opposite page, causing the happy couple to shed a tear. If your photographs are not a suitable size to trace off, and treat them gently if you do, enlarge them at a local photocopying shop. The board is made from thin plywood with notches cut out where the spine falls. I then covered it with blue-sticky-backed plastic followed by a wide strip of leather-effect sticky-backed plastic down the middle and a piece on each corner for the binding.

INGREDIENTS
25 × 20 cm (10 × 8 inch) oblong rich fruit cake, using quantity for 23 cm (9 inch) square (p.17)

apricot glaze (p.17)

1 kg (2 lb 4 oz) marzipan (p.15)

icing sugar for dusting

1 kg (2 lb 4 oz) fondant icing (p.15)

basic paste food colours: brown, blue, black

OTHER MATERIALS
56 × 25 cm (22 × 10 inch) thin hardboard or cut-down cake board, covered in blue and then leather-effect sticky-back plastic

SPECIAL EQUIPMENT
icing smoothers

ruler

tracing paper

soft pencil

fine artist's paint brush

absorbent kitchen paper

NOTE: Allow at least 1 day extra preparation time for marzipan to dry.

1 Trim the cake level then cut in half horizontally to give two shallow cakes. Cut one end of each cake at an angle for the edges of the pages, then carve into the opposite ends at an angle to shape the binding at the spine (see diagram). Position both cakes, joined together, on the cake board and brush them all over with apricot glaze.

2 Cover with marzipan in sections as for a square cake (p.22), cutting eight strips to cover the sides (tucking the inner ends in under the spine) and one long piece to cover the top, pressing it into the centre of the book with the back of a knife. Roll the top lightly with a rolling pin to flatten, smooth all the joins together with the flat blade of a knife and leave to dry for at least 24 hours.

3 Colour 900 g (2 lb) of the fondant beige, reserve 25 g (1 oz) and use the rest to cover the cake in sections as with the marzipan, rolling out the pieces on an icing sugar dusted surface and cutting to size with a sharp knife. Smooth all over with your hands or icing smoothers then press the back of a knife around the sides of the fondant to make it look like pages.

4 Colour the reserved 25 g (1 oz) beige fondant a darker shade of brown. Using half of it, make two small semi-circles to tuck in under the spine at the top and bottom to neaten. Keep the rest to make the picture corners.

5 Colour 15 g (½ oz) of the fondant blue, roll out and cut a strip 1 × 25 cm (½ × 10 inches). Snip along one end to make a fringe and position it on the cake to make the bookmark, tucking into the binding at the top of the cake.

6 Roll out the remaining white fondant fairly thin on an icing sugar dusted surface and cut out two rectangles (use a ruler), 11.5 × 16.5 cm (4½ × 6½ inches). Fix these to the cake in the centre of each page with a very little water. Leave to dry for 1 hour.

7 Trace your chosen photographs onto tracing paper, turn over and go over the lines with a soft pencil, then turn back and trace off onto the white picture areas on the cake. Using a plate as a palette, mix black paste food colour with various amounts of water to make shades of grey and paint the photographs with a fine paint brush, following the traced outlines. Keeping an eye on the original photograph, start working gingerly on the light areas then work towards the darker areas and finally fill in the details. Remember that you can always add colour but not remove it (except for small highlights, which can be scratched out or painted in with opaque white if necessary, but this does make the surface uneven). Blot the brush on absorbent kitchen paper as necessary.

8 Make a template for the picture corners with a small piece of paper, then roll out the reserved brown fondant on an icing sugar dusted board. With a sharp knife, cut round the template eight times and press the pieces into place on the corners of the photographs.

9 Finally, you may like to a paint message under the pictures with black paste colour.

RIVIA

*Who played Mike Baldwin's father in the
long-running TV soap Coronation Street?
If you know the answer to this question, you
are either a Sam Kydd fan (like myself) or a
trivia addict. Played by smart alecks of all
ages and interests, this game must be in
almost every household by now. Everyone
has their own name for the pieces – triangles,
cheeses, pies – perhaps after this they will be
called slices of cake!
A light fruit cake made with multi-coloured
cherries reflects the colourful exterior.*

INGREDIENTS

18 cm (7 inch) round light fruit cake (p.8)

450 g (1 lb) marzipan (p.15)

apricot glaze (p.17)

950 g (2 lb 2 oz) fondant icing (p.15)

*basic paste food colours: yellow, pink, green, blue,
brown, orange*

icing sugar for dusting

OTHER MATERIALS

18 cm (7 inch) round cake board

Trivial Pursuits game board for serving (optional!)

SPECIAL EQUIPMENT

non-stick baking paper

soft pencil

tracing paper

thick paper or thin card

scissors

ruler

NOTE: Allow at least 1 day extra preparation time for
marzipan to dry.

1 Place the cake board on a large sheet of non-stick paper. Trim the cake level if necessary, place upside down on the board and fill any gaps around the bottom with a little marzipan. Brush the cake all over with apricot glaze and cover with marzipan in the usual way (p.21), extending it over the sides of the cake board as well. Leave to dry for at least 24 hours.

2 Colour the fondant icing in the following quantities, keeping each piece wrapped until needed: 75 g (3 oz) each of yellow, pink, green, blue and beige, and the remainder orange.

3 Trace the triangle template shown overleaf with a pencil onto tracing paper, transfer onto thick paper or thin card and cut out.

4 Dampen the top of the cake with a little water on your fingers. On an icing sugar dusted surface, roll out the fondant one colour at a time to roughly the size of the triangle template. Place the template card on top of the fondant and cut to the exact shape with a knife. Lay the five pieces over the top of the cake, butting them together and finishing with the sixth segment made from 75 g (3 oz) of the orange fondant. Lightly roll the top of the cake with a rolling pin to level the fondant, then cut out strips approximately 1 cm (½ inch) wide between each segment, using a knife against a ruler and pulling the fondant out to make a channel between each colour.

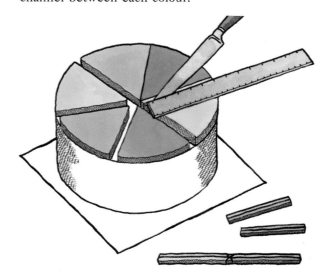

5 On an icing sugar dusted surface, roll out 100 g (4 oz) of the orange fondant into a sausage approximately 19 cm (7½ inches) long. Flatten this with a rolling pin to make a strip approximately 3 cm (1¼ inches) wide, and slice this into three strips 1 cm (½ inch) wide.

Ease one strip into one of the channels right across the cake and cut the other strips in half at an angle to fit in the other channels and make a good join at the centre. Trim neatly.

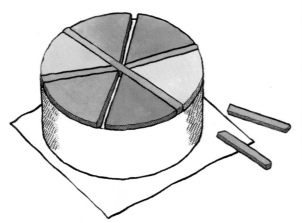

6 Dampen the sides of the cake as before. Measure the depth of the cake. On an icing sugar dusted surface, roll out the remaining orange fondant to make a strip approximately 55 cm (22 inches) long – the circumference of the cake – and as wide as the cake is deep. Trim the edges neatly against a ruler and wrap the strip around the cake. Smooth together the join, tidy the bottom edge and smooth all round with icing smoothers or a glass tumbler. Leave to dry for a couple of hours then carefully slide the cake with its board off the paper onto the game board.

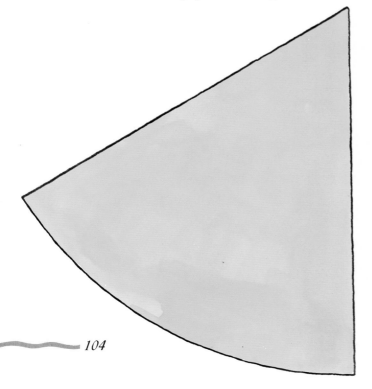

*t*UTTI FRUTTI

Johnny will be good if you make him a cake of his favourite brothel creepers, part of the garb of the true Teddy Boy. The style, like the music, will never die: – greased-up quiff, bootlace tie, drape suit, fluorescent socks and chunky crepe-soled shoes. It is still remembered with affection and regret by those whose mum wouldn't let them have an outfit way back then.

INGREDIENTS
25 × 20 cm (10 × 8 inch) oblong rich fruit cake, using quantity for 23 cm (9 inch) square (p.7)
1 kg (2 lb 4 oz) marzipan (p.15)
apricot glaze (p.17)
icing sugar for dusting
1.5 kg (3 lb 6 oz) fondant icing (p.15)
basic paste food colours: yellow, black, orange, green
liquorice shoelaces
OTHER MATERIALS
30 cm (12 inch) square cake board (drum), covered with strips of mirror tiles
SPECIAL EQUIPMENT
pencil
greaseproof paper
scissors
non-stick baking paper
round skewer or knitting needle
fine artist's paint brush

NOTE: Allow at least 1 day extra preparation time for marzipan to dry.

1 Trace the template on page 110 onto grease-proof paper and cut out. Alternatively draw round a shoe and cut out approximately 1 cm (½ inch) inside of this line to make a template. (Draw round the shape of the body of the shoe and not just the sole, as you will cut away the instep later to shape the shoe.)

2 Cut the top of the cake to level it a bit and turn it over. Place the template on one side of the cake and use it as a guide to cut out one shoe: turn the template over and cut out the other shoe from the other side of the cake. Turn both shoe cakes over and place on a sheet of non-stick baking paper.

3 Carve the shoes into shape, cutting into the bottom inside of each shoe to make the instep. Add extra points of marzipan to the toes and, if needed, thick semi-circular slabs for the top of the fronts where the tongue is. When you are happy with the shape, brush the cakes all over with apricot glaze. Divide the remaining marzipan in two. On an icing sugar dusted surface, roll out a large piece of the marzipan to cover each shoe. Lay the marzipan over each cake in turn and smooth down all over with your hands. Trim neatly round the bottom and leave to dry for at least 24 hours.

4 Position the cakes on the cake board, slightly apart. Colour 250 g (9 oz) of the fondant icing cream. Divide this in two and roll out each piece on an icing sugar dusted surface to an area large enough to cover the front area of each shoe in one piece, including the tongue. Place on, tuck the top flap of icing over the tongue of the shoe, then cut to the required shape.

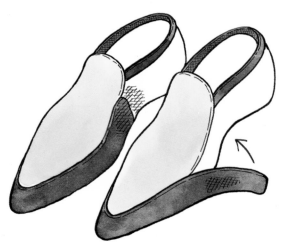

5 Colour 1 kg (2 lb 4 oz) of the fondant black and reserve 300 g (11 oz) of this, tightly wrapped. Using 75 g (3 oz) black icing, make two sausages each approximately 33 cm (13 inches) long and press one around the top rim of each shoe to build up the sides and back a little. On an icing sugar dusted surface, roll out 100 g (4 oz) more black fondant and cut out two strips for each shoe, approximately 30 × 5 cm (12 × 2 inches). Attach the strips to the front of each shoe with a little water, joining them together at the toe, butting them up to the cream fondant and, if necessary, trimming around the base.

6 Hold a piece of greaseproof paper against the outside of one cake shoe. With a pencil, sketch or trace the template overleaf to cover the back half and protruding frontpiece (where the laces are) in one piece, and cut out with scissors. On an icing sugar dusted surface, roll out half the remaining black fondant. Use the template as a guide to cut out one shoe side, then turn the template over and cut out another. Make lace holes in the frontpieces with a skewer or knitting needle. Dampen the outsides of the shoes with a little water on your fingers then dry your hands. Lift the fondant pieces onto the shoes and smooth on with your hands. Now check the template for size on the *inside* of one shoe, modifying if necessary, and cut out two pieces as before from the (rolled-out) remaining black fondant, remembering to cut the lace holes. Dampen the insides of the cake shoes and attach these cut-out pieces as before. Make sure the top edges are neat and smooth together the joins at the back.

7 To make the soles, roll out the reserved 300 g (11 oz) black fondant, and cut out two thick strips about 2.5 cm (1 inch) wide and long enough to go right round the base of each cake shoe. Wrap these strips around the edge, attaching them with a little water; immediately press a skewer or knitting needle repeatedly around the sides to give a vertically ridged effect.

8 With a fine artist's paint brush and black paste food colour, paint irregular spots on the cream fronts of the shoes and then lightly brush fine lines around the edges of the spots to give a fake fur effect.

9 With the point of a skewer or knitting needle, make holes in the underlying cream fondant through the black lace holes. Cut short lengths of liquorice shoelace and press them into these holes, crisscrossing each other to look like real laces.

10 Colour the remaining fondant icing to make the socks. I chose to divide this in half and have one orange and one lime green sock, but you can make them both the same colour if you wish. Roll out each piece on an icing sugar dusted surface to a rough oval shape then crumple up and tuck into the top of each shoe.

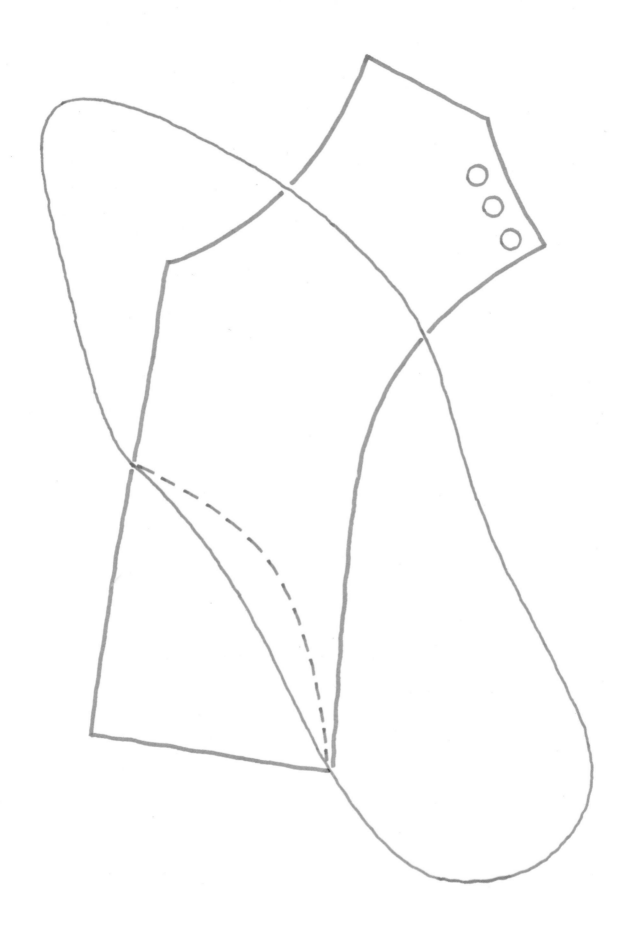

DECORATION WITH MASK

In his later years and with failing health, the French artist Henri Matisse (1869–1954) gradually gave up painting in favour of making large collages of cut paper. Studio assistants produced a stockpile of bright gouache-painted paper and he cut out different shapes with scissors, moving the pieces around until he was happy with the composition. This work of strong colours and simple shapes has been the inspiration for a lot of recent graphic and fabric design. A floral cake with a difference, this is simple to make and depends for its success on sharp lines and clean work. Use a sharp craft knife to cut out the fondant icing, wiping and drying the blade frequently to prevent a build-up of icing.

INGREDIENTS

25 cm (10 inch) square light fruit cake (p.8)
apricot glaze (p.17)
1 kg (2 lb 4 oz) marzipan (p.15)
icing sugar for dusting
1 kg (2 lb 4 oz) fondant icing (p.15)
basic paste food colours: blue, red, pink, green, yellow

OTHER MATERIALS

30 cm (12 inch) square cake board (drum), covered with black sticky-back plastic

SPECIAL EQUIPMENT

icing smoothers
tracing paper
pencil
thin card
scissors
medium artist's paint brush
ruler
small round cutter or lid

NOTE: Allow at least 1 day extra preparation time for marzipan to dry.

1 Level the top of the cake, position upside down in the centre of the cake board and cover with marzipan, using apricot glaze to stick (p.21). Leave to dry for at least 24 hours.

2 On an icing sugar dusted surface, roll out 800 g (1 lb 12 oz) of the white fondant to make a 40 cm (16 inch) square. Supporting it with the rolling pin, lay the icing over the cake and lightly roll over the top. Smooth down the sides with your hands, trim the corners and work together the joins. Trim round the bottom neatly and, if you have them, smooth all over with icing smoothers to sharpen and neaten the corners of the cake.

3 Gather up any offcuts and add them to the remaining fondant. Colour 75 g (3 oz) blue, divide the remainder into four and colour these pieces red, pink, green and yellow. Keep each piece wrapped separately to prevent drying out.

4 Trace the templates (overleaf) on to tracing paper, transfer onto thin card and cut out with scissors. Roll out the coloured fondant fairly thinly on an icing sugar dusted surface, a little at a time, and with a sharp knife cut out flower petal shapes using the card templates as guides.

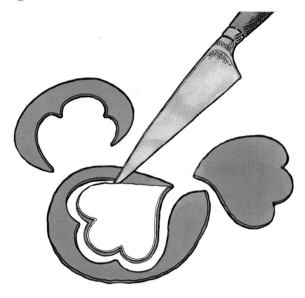

5 Lay the petals lightly on the top of the cake, securing with a dampened brush when you are happy with their position. Place two flowers on each side of the cake, again attaching them with a little water. Cut out thin blue fondant strips against a ruler for a good straight edge, and semi-circles with a cutter or small lid to make the 'column' design at both ends of each side of the cake, attaching with a little water as before.

6 Roll out thin sausages of blue fondant, bend and position in the middle of the cake in a face design and flatten slightly. Make the other small blobs between the flowers in the same way, attaching with a little water.

CAKOFAX

Yuppies may come and Porsches may go but the Filofax is here to stay! Make this cake to celebrate a birthday, toast a business success or mourn the loss of one of these personal organizers, which would be a dark day indeed for the sorrowful owner whose entire 'life' has suddenly slipped out of his or her hands.

Since you only use half of the sponge cake in this recipe, you may feel there is not enough actual cake in this for your party, so you could construct the Cakofax on top of a larger square or round cake covered with fondant icing to resemble part of a desk top — or, perhaps more pertinent, a wine bar table top.

INGREDIENTS

18 cm (7 inch) square shallow chocolate sponge cake (p.9), using quantity for 15 cm (6 inch) square

apricot glaze (p.17)

250 g (9 oz) fondant icing (p.15)

icing sugar for dusting

200 g (7 oz) chewy chocolate covering made with dark chocolate (p.16)

basic paste food colours: yellow, pink, black

silver lustre powder

OTHER MATERIALS

23 × 18 cm (9 × 7 inch) cake board, cut from a 23 cm (9 inch) square and then covered with grey sticky-back plastic

wooden skewer

SPECIAL EQUIPMENT

fine artist's paint brush

non-stick baking paper

ruler

1 Cut the cake in half vertically and trim off the top and bottom crusts from one half (you will not need the other half). Position on the cake board so that it is slightly off centre and brush with apricot glaze.

2 Colour 50 g (2 oz) of the fondant yellow and 50 g (2 oz) pink. On an icing sugar dusted surface, roll out each fondant and then 75 g (3 oz) of the remaining white fondant to long sausages that will fit right round the sides of the cake (approximately 50 cm/20 inches long). Flatten these to form strips and wrap round the sides of the cake a colour at a time to build up the effect of coloured pages. Make sure the joins are on the spine side of the cake so that they will be completely hidden.

3 Cut a thin diagonal slot in the fondant on the long open side of the Cakofax, 3 mm (⅛ inch) wide, and pull away the thin strip of icing. Roll out 15 g (½ oz) more white fondant to make a strip approximately 1 cm (½ inch) wide, 16 cm (6½ inches) long and 3 mm (⅛ inch) thick; insert it sideways into the slot so that it protrudes – a little water will help it stick if it refuses. With a very sharp knife, cut the length of strip into 13 equal parts and gently press each piece horizontal with a flat knife. Leave to dry for at least 30 minutes and then paint on the index letters with a fine paint brush and black food colouring.

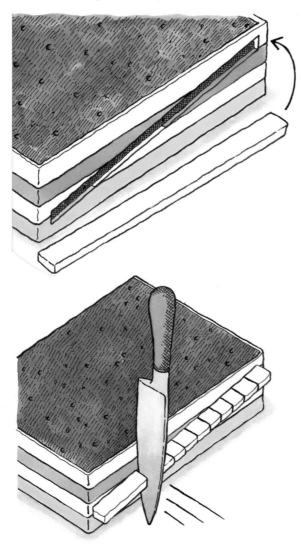

4 Crumple up a sheet of non-stick baking paper and smooth out again. Place all the chewy chocolate covering on another sheet of non-stick baking paper and place the crumpled non-stick baking paper on top. Roll out until the chocolate is no more than 3 mm (⅛ inch) thick – the crumpled paper will give the icing a leather-grained effect. With a sharp knife and ruler, cut out a piece in the shape of a three-sided frame to fit around the bottom of the cake (the 'back cover' of your Cakofax). Position it on the cake board, butting it up to the bottom edge of the cake neatly all the way round. Trim the outside of the chewy chocolate frame straight so it is about 1 cm (½ inch) wide.

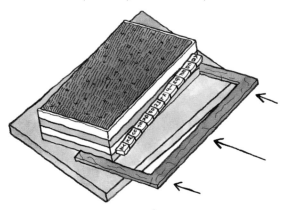

5 Gather up all the chewy chocolate covering and roll out again under the sheet of crumpled non-stick paper as before. Cut out a rectangular piece approximately 19 × 16 cm (7½ × 6½ inches) and lay this over the top of the cake and round the spine. Curve the spine so that it doesn't touch the side of the cake, to make the front cover. The covering should extend slightly over the edge of the cake all the way round, like the back cover underneath.

6 Colour half the remaining fondant black and the other half grey. Mould a pen shape around a dampened wooden skewer with the black fondant and use a little grey fondant to make a clip. Position the pen along the long side of the back cover, and use an offcut of the 'leathered' chewy chocolate covering to make a strip (approximately 2.5 × 9 cm/1 × 3½ inches), to keep the Cakofax closed. To attach the strip, lift the chewy chocolate back cover up in the centre on that side, tuck the strap piece

under and fold it over gently to lie on the top of the cake. Use a little of the grey and black fondant to make a round press stud on the top of the strap.

7 Use the remaining grey fondant to make the ring binding mechanism inside the spine: just tuck a small round-ended strip inside the spine at the top and bottom, and then paint all the grey fondant with silver lustre powder mixed with a little water for a metallic finish.

8 Finally, rub a little icing sugar into the cover to enhance the leather grain effect and then brush off any excess.

P.O.S.H

The advent of jet travel has diminished the number of ocean liners sailing the high seas but not the image of style, affluence and adventure that they conjure up in most minds. Romantic dreams of dinner with the captain and moonlit strolls around the deck in warmer climes is what keeps many football pools punters filling in their coupons with those little crosses throughout our miserable winters.

Streamlining and simplifying the shapes in the style of 1930s posters, and tapering the cake towards the back give the impression of size and grandeur. The board is tapered too – I cut down a silver cake board and re-covered it but you could make it from chipboard or several layers of corrugated cardboard covered with silver paper.

INGREDIENTS

25 cm (10 inch) square rich fruit cake (p.7)
apricot glaze (p.17)
750 g (1 lb 10 oz) marzipan (p.15)
icing sugar for dusting
750 g (1 lb 10 oz) fondant icing (p.15)
basic paste food colours: black, red, blue, green

OTHER MATERIALS

33 cm (13 inch) square cake board (drum), cut on two sides to form a tapering oblong (15 cm/6 inches wide at one end and 7.5 cm/3 inches wide at the other), and then covered with silver cake board paper

SPECIAL EQUIPMENT

icing smoothers
non-stick baking paper
fine artist's paint brush

NOTE: Allow at least 1 day extra preparation time for marzipan to dry.

1 Carve out a boat shape from the cake, cutting vertically through the square as shown in the diagram. Then carve the back of the cake down so that the whole outline slopes towards the back, following the angle of the raised front of the ship.

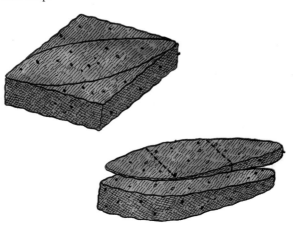

2 Take two wedge-shaped offcuts and place on the boat cake to build up the front and top as shown, sticking them down with apricot glaze. Also carve into the bottom of the ship along both sides so that the cake is narrower at the base than the top. Position the cake on the board and brush all over with apricot glaze.

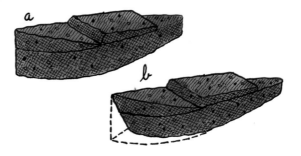

3 Use a little of the marzipan to build up the point at the front of the cake then, working in sections, roll out and cover the cake with all the marzipan. Use approximately a third to cover each side and the remaining third for the top. Roll out the marzipan on an icing sugar dusted surface, cut roughly to shape then lift carefully onto the cake, smoothing into the angles with your hands and working together joins with the flat blade of a knife to give a neat finish. Leave to dry for at least 24 hours.

4 Colour 250 g (9 oz) of the fondant black and, reserving 15 g (½ oz) of this for the funnel tops and the anchor, divide it in two. Dampen the sides of the cake with a little water on your fingers. On an icing sugar dusted surface, roll out one piece of black fondant at a time roughly to the shape of the side of the boat, cut to size, and carefully apply to one side of the cake. When covered, smooth the joins together front and back with your fingers and polish all over with the palms of your hands or with icing smoothers. With a knife, cut the black fondant 1 cm (½ inch) from the top of the sides of the cake in a smooth straight line all the way round, and remove any fondant above this line. Add these offcuts to the reserved 15 g (½ oz). Wash your hands thoroughly.

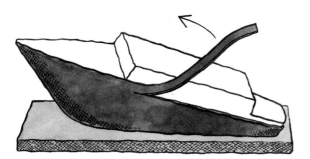

5 Cover the top of the cake with 150 g (5½ oz) of the white fondant. Work in sections, rolling the pieces roughly to shape on an icing sugar dusted surface then cutting to size and applying to the cake with a little water. Start with triangular shapes to cover the front and back decks, a thin strip to cover the front of the upper deck, a tapering oblong to cover each side of the upper deck (which extends down to the black fondant at the bottom) and lastly a piece to cover the top of the upper deck, curved at the front.

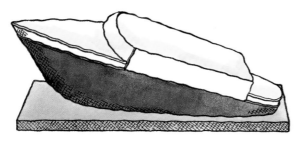

6 Make the very top deck by rolling out a slab of 100 g (4 oz) white fondant; thick at the front and tapering to thin at the back. Cut to size and place towards the front of the upper deck of the cake.

7 Using 50 g (2 oz) of white fondant, roll out four tapering strips to fit in the gaps round the front and back edge of the ship above the black line; cut the edges straight and apply with a little water, butting up to the black fondant and making the top stand proud of the top of the cake a little. Smooth together the join where these strips meet the other white icing at the top of the cake.

8 Colour 100 g (4 oz) fondant red and make three funnels of decreasing height and thickness. Each funnel is a slightly flattened sausage shape, cut at an angle at the top and finished off with a piece of reserved black fondant. Place a piece of non-stick baking paper on top of the cake and try the funnels for size and positioning before finally removing the paper and attaching them. Make a small black anchor for the front end of the ship.

9 With a fine paint brush and black food colouring, paint on a name, portholes and windows around the white fondant, positioning these closer together towards the back to accentuate the perspective effect.

10 Reserve a small piece of the remaining fondant and colour the rest bluey-green. If you do not mix the colours in thoroughly you will get an interesting watery effect. Divide the fondant in two and roll out each piece large enough to easily cover each side of the cake drum. Place the fondant sea over the board, folding up at the front to look like waves; butt the inner edge of the fondant sea up to the cake and bend back the upper edges into points for the breaking water. Trim the fondant around the sides of the cake drum in a wavy line. Finally, roll pieces of the remaining white fondant and apply to the tops of the bluey-green fondant waves to look like sea foam.

*t*EA CAKE

Drinking tea has always been a British institution. Morning, noon and night, according to an old popular song, we as a nation drink gallons of the stuff. All sorts of people would welcome this treat of tea and cake, especially if the china matched their own or conveyed a message in the design of lucky shamrocks, horseshoes, love hearts or flowers.

The shape of this teapot was made by cooking the cake in each half of a spherical metal rice steamer lined with foil and greaseproof paper, but you could make other designs with a pudding basin cake or round cakes which have been cut to shape.

INGREDIENTS
quantity for 18 cm (7 inch) square rich fruit cake (p.7), divided between a rice steamer and a half-filled 425 g (15 oz) can
1 kg (2 lb 4 oz) fondant icing (p.15)
icing sugar for dusting
apricot glaze (p.17)
500 g (1 lb 2 oz) marzipan (p.15)
basic paste food colours: green, brown, yellow

OTHER MATERIALS
wooden skewer
wooden tea tray

SPECIAL EQUIPMENT
saucer
non-stick baking paper
small spice jars
fine artist's paint brush
carrot (for printing)
petal shape cutter
flat plate

NOTE: Allow at least 1 day extra preparation time for icing and marzipan to dry.

1 Colour 750 g (1 lb 10 oz) of the fondant icing pale green, and reserve 650 g (1 lb 7 oz) of it, tightly wrapped. Dust a saucer thoroughly with icing sugar, and roll out the remaining green fondant into a circle large enough to fit the saucer. Lay it in the saucer, smoothing down well and trimming the edges. Leave to dry in a warm place such as an airing cupboard for at least 24 hours.

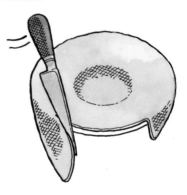

2 Level the top of the hemispherical cakes a little and brush with apricot glaze. Roll 50 g (2 oz) of the marzipan into a circle on an icing sugar dusted surface and sandwich between the two cakes. Brush the whole cake with apricot glaze, roll the remaining marzipan out into a large circle and lift over the sphere of cake, smoothing it down the sides with your hands and cutting off excess folds. Roll the whole cake around on an icing sugar dusted surface to smooth the surface, and work the joins together. Press the cake onto a small sheet of non-stick baking paper to give it a small flat base.

3 Carve the other cake roughly into the shape of a cup, taking advantage of the flat bottom of the cake to produce the smooth top. Gather together the offcuts of marzipan and roll out a strip to go round the side of the cup cake, and attach with apricot glaze. Roll out a small circle to cover the top, attach with apricot glaze and work the join together firmly. Place on a small piece of non-stick baking paper and leave both cakes to dry for at least 24 hours.

4 Colour 25 g (1 oz) of the remaining fondant a 'tea' colour, roll out a small circle on an icing sugar dusted surface, and use to cover the top of the cup cake. Roll out 75 g (3 oz) of the reserved pale green fondant into a strip long enough to go round the cup cake and wide enough to cover the sides and also stand 5 mm (¼ inch) above the top. Attach to the side of the cup with a little water, smoothing together the join and round the bottom. Mould a handle from 25 g (1 oz) of the pale green fondant, attach with a little water and leave to dry supported by a small jar covered with a piece of non-stick paper.

5 Dampen the spherical cake all over with a very little water. On an icing sugar dusted surface roll out 350 g (12 oz) more of the pale green fondant to make a large circle (approximately 40 cm/16 inches diameter) and lift it over the cake. Smooth down all round with your hands and cut off any excess folds, working the joins together well. Trim neatly round the bottom and use the offcuts to roll a pencil-thick sausage approximately 28 cm (11 inches) long and then a knob for the top. Attach the sausage round the top with a little water to make a rim and press down the fondant just inside this with the end of a spoon to make a groove so that the top looks like a separate lid. Attach the knob to the top with a little water.

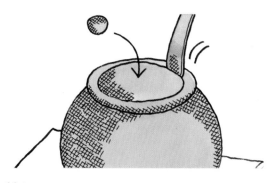

6 With half the remaining pale green fondant (about 100 g/4 oz), model a spout around a dampened wooden skewer, leaving the point sticking out to attach it to the cake. Leave to dry a little. Meanwhile, mould a teapot handle from the other half of the fondant and attach it firmly to the cake with a little water. Support it while drying with jars covered with non-stick baking paper. Insert the spout skewer into the cake and attach the spout with a little water. Prop up as before with non-stick paper on a jar and leave to dry for 1 hour.

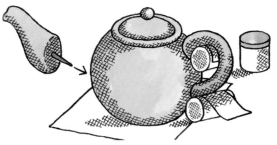

7 Using a paint brush and paste food colours, paint on the design of your choice or print one. To print a design, use a fine artist's brush and green food colouring to paint the line on the saucer and the top of the teapot. Cut a carrot straight across and with a small sharp knife cut your design in the end of it to make a simple printing block. Dip this in a strong solution of paste food colour and test out by printing first on paper. You will soon be able to judge how much it needs blotting before printing onto the cup and teapot cakes, as too much colour will give a blotted effect. Retouch any holes in the printed designs with a paint brush. Leave for 1 hour to dry or use a hairdryer.

8 Colour the remaining fondant icing cream and roll out on an icing sugar dusted surface to fit your wooden tea tray. Cut out an oval or rectangle shape and, supporting with the rolling pin, lift it onto the tray. With the petal shape cutter, cut out flower shapes, lifting out the fondant pieces so that the tray can be seen through. Clean away any icing sugar.

9 Place a flat plate over the fondant saucer, upturn and carefully lift off the real saucer. Brush any excess icing sugar off the bottom of the fondant saucer and carefully place it right way up on the tray cloth. Place the teapot, cup and saucer on the cloth.

*P*INK LADY

I have had many requests for nudes on cakes, mostly from men, so here is a reasonably tasteful one which I have made before for a sculptress.

Watching a grown man decide how to cut a cake like this is pathetically funny. 'Which bit shall we eat first?' he will utter, grinning like a schoolboy. The photographer's four-year-old son ate the extended foot first but that was the easiest piece to pinch while dad's back was turned.

Look at real sculptures in the park, town square or museum and get someone to pose for you (not necessarily nude or female!) to get the basic proportions of the figure; it is much easier than trying to work from photographs. If you are not happy with the way some parts turn out, just cover them with fondant drapery as I did – it all adds to the classical look!

INGREDIENTS
23 cm (9 inch) square rich fruit cake (p.7)
apricot glaze (p.17)
750 g (1 lb 10 oz) marzipan (p.15)
icing sugar for dusting
1 kg (2 lb 4 oz) fondant icing (p.15)
basic paste food colours: pink, yellow

OTHER MATERIALS
28 × 18 cm (11 × 7 inch) cake board (drum), cut from a 28 cm (11 inch) square and then covered with silver cake board paper
cocktail stick

SPECIAL EQUIPMENT
palette knife
cocktail stick, skewer, or modelling tools
fine artist's paint brush
icing smoother

NOTE: Allow at least 1 day extra preparation time for marzipan to dry.

1 Cut the fruit cake vertically in half, trim the top of one half level and position it on the cake board; brush all over with apricot glaze. Using 400 g (14 oz) of the marzipan rolled out on an icing sugar dusted surface, cover the cake in the usual way for a square cake (p.22).

2 Roughly carve the remaining half of cake into the shape of a figure leaning on a heap of cushions, leaving off the head, arms, feet and other small details – just make sure you have cut away enough, as you can always build the shape up with fondant but it is harder to remove cake once it is covered with marzipan. Position the figure on top of the other cake and brush with apricot glaze.

3 On an icing sugar dusted surface, roll out the remaining marzipan to an area large enough to cover the figure. Carefully lift the marzipan onto the cake and smooth down all over. Cut away folds, patch up any holes and work the joins together with the flat blade of a knife. Trim the lower edge of the figure tidily around the base and leave to dry for at least 24 hours.

4 Colour half the fondant icing pale pink. Push a dampened cocktail stick into the top of the figure cake to support the head. Take a small piece of pink fondant and push it onto the cocktail stick for the basis of the neck and another ball (smaller than you want the finished head to be) for the basis of the head. Build up the front knee and the breasts with a little more fondant, smoothing carefully into the marzipan.

5 Colour half of the remaining white fondant (about 250 g/9 oz) a deeper shade of pink and the rest a peachy colour. Roll sausages of each of the three shades of fondant – pale pink, deep pink and peach – and lay them randomly together on an icing sugar dusted surface.

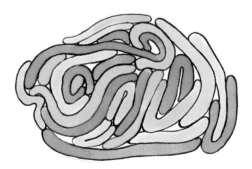

6 Roll out the sausages fairly thickly with a rolling pin to give a slightly marbled effect. If there are any areas that are not well marbled, pull them out, push in other pieces torn from the edges, fold up and roll again. Add some extra pink colour with a cocktail stick to make the veining, and keep working the fondant until you achieve an overall marbled effect.

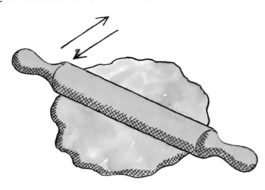

7 Cut off about a quarter of the marbled icing (place the rest, lightly folded, in a plastic bag to prevent drying out) and roll out more thinly on an icing sugar dusted surface to an area large enough to cover the figure and top of the plinth cake. Lay it carefully on the cake, cutting a slit to pull over the head. Smooth down all over with your hands, easing into the curves, cutting off any excess folds and working the joins together. Push the fondant well in under the figure and trim neatly at the edge of the plinth cake.

8 Roll out half of the remaining fondant and cut rectangular pieces to fit all the sides of the plinth cake and the top of the cake board. (Cut two pieces 23 × 7.5 cm/9 × 3 inches, and two pieces 11.5 × 7.5 cm/4½ × 3 inches.) Dampen the sides of this base cake with a little water on your fingers, dry your hands and attach the fondant, smoothing all over with the icing smoother. Butt the other pieces up to the edge of the cake on the board, smooth together the joins and trim away neatly round the edge of the cake board.

Gather up the offcuts and, together with half again of the reserved marbled fondant, mould and attach the foot, arms, hands and cushions, working in the joins.

9 Mould the neck and face with all its features like a mask out of a thick, flat piece of fondant, and wrap it around the head, smoothing it on. Sharpen up the features with a cocktail stick, skewer or modelling tools. Use tiny rolls of fondant to make the hair, securing them on with a dampened brush.

10 Roll out thinly pieces of the remaining fondant on an icing sugar dusted surface for the swags around the plinth and the drapery on the figure. For the swags, pinch little oblongs of fondant into folds, pulling together at each end and securing around the plinth with a little water. Cover the joins with tiny balls of fondant. For the drapery, simply roll out very thin lengths of fondant, scrunch up a bit into folds and lay carefully over the figure where required, securing with a dampened paint brush.

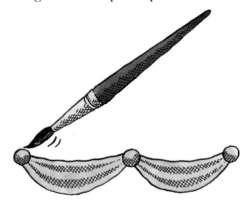

JAMITYVILLE

*'Small detached cottage. Original features,
unusual aspect. Sitting tenant in the attic,
seldom seen. View before sunset.'*
*When you move house you can't be sure what
you are getting with the bricks and mortar.*
*This haunted hovel is a send-up of the
spectres of damp and worm that a surveyor
seeks and a new homeowner dreads. Either
would be glad to cut into this cake and
find a reassuringly well made and
'tasteful' interior.*
*Decorate this cake quickly to keep the sponge
cake fresh and so as not to get too bogged
down in detail – there is a large area to cover
with a fairly repetitious design of windows
and bricks and you can get very bored
with it.*
*I brought the black sugar crystals in a sweet
shop but, if you can't get this, use dark
brown sugar or toasted desiccated coconut.*

INGREDIENTS

two 18 cm (7 inch) square sponge cakes (p.9)
15 cm (6 inch) square sponge cake (p.9)
apricot glaze (p.17)
150 g (5½ oz) buttercream (p.17)
1.8 kg (4 lb) fondant icing (p.15)
basic paste food colours: red, brown, black, yellow
icing sugar for dusting
100 g (4 oz) black sugar crystals

OTHER MATERIALS

25 cm (10 inch) square cake board (drum), covered with dark sticky-back plastic
cocktail sticks

SPECIAL EQUIPMENT

non-stick baking paper
ruler
medium artist's paint brush

1 If necessary, trim the cakes level. Brush the top of both the 18 cm (7 inch) cakes with apricot glaze, place one on top of the other and then place the 15 cm (6 inch) cake centrally on top to create a three-tiered structure. Carve the sides in a gentle outwards curve, turn the whole cake upside down so it is widest at the top and position at the back of the cake board.

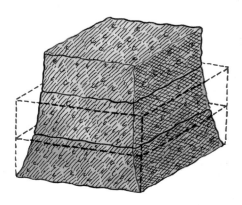

2 Cut the sides of the new top cake off at an angle for the roof and attach these pieces to the top with some buttercream, to add to the cake's height. Use more buttercream to plaster up any holes and gaps around the cake, and then brush all over with apricot glaze.

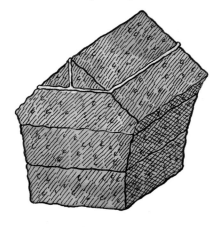

3 Colour 850 g (1 lb 14 oz) of the fondant a reddish-brown, reserve 150 g (5½ oz) of it tightly wrapped and use the rest to cover the walls of the cake house: divide this quantity

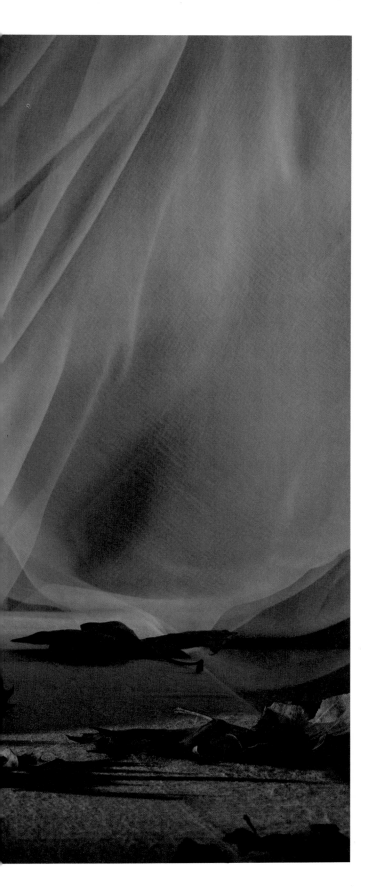

roughly into four and roll out each piece on an icing sugar dusted surface to fit each side (judge this by eye or measure the cake). Lift the pieces carefully onto the cake, folding any excess over the top and trimming neatly at the bottom. Spead any remaining buttercream over the roof area to make it even.

4 Fold up pieces of non-stick paper to make fairly stiff strips and place them around edges of the roof so that they extend beyond it all the way round, forming eaves.

5 Colour 350 g (12 oz) of the fondant black and roll out 300 g (11 oz) of it on an icing sugar dusted surface to a large rectangle to cover the roof, including the paper eaves. Cut out against a ruler for straight edges and lay over the roof, folding over the top ridge. Mark on tiles with a knife.

6 Roll out the remaining black fondant and cut out a rectangle approximately 3 × 1.5 cm (1¼ × ½ inch). Fold this in half widthways down the middle for the chimney roof and leave to dry.

7 Use 75 g (3 oz) of the reserved reddish-brown fondant to mould an oblong, thick slab for the chimney stack and attach it to the side of the roof cake with a cocktail stick set at a slight angle. Colour the rest of the reserved fondant a darker shade of brown. Use a little of this darker brown fondant to make a chimney, pressing a face into it with a cocktail stick before attaching to the top of the chimney stack with a little water. Use the rest of the dark brown fondant to roll and cut out front and back doors. Press a knife into the fondant to make a panel design on the doors and attach with a little water.

8 Push a cocktail stick into the cake above the front door and roll out, cut out and fold a thin triangle of black fondant to form a porch; fit this over the cocktail stick with a little water.

9 Colour 200 g (7 oz) of fondant light grey. Don't bother to work in the colour too well as a smeary look is effective. Roll out the fondant fairly thinly on an icing sugar dusted surface and, freehand, cut out the window shapes; cut away and insert pieces of black fondant in the main front window pieces before attaching the windows to the cake with a dampened paint brush. With grey offcuts, make two tiny letter-boxes and attach to the doors.

10 Pull out the pieces of non-stick paper supporting the roof, which should be dry enough by now.

11 Colour the remaining fondant icing cream and make the other features on the cake, attaching them with a dampened brush. Roll out and cut straight pieces for the window sills, doorsteps and pieces under the eaves (these can be marked with the tip of a knife to make a ridged design before attaching), and roll thin sausages to make window frames. Cut small, fairly thin rectangles to go along the top of the roof and up the corners of the side walls. Mould a gargoyle shape around one end of a damp cocktail stick and push into place at the top of the roof, and another smaller one to go above the front door. Attach the now fairly dry black roof to the chimney.

12 Mix a little of the black sugar crystals with some icing sugar and spoon onto the drum to make the path. Spoon the rest of the sugar all around the board, pushing it up to the cake.

ON THE TILES

In Roman floor mosaics, the two-handled cup or chalice was the symbol of generosity and hospitality, a suitable motif for a cake. Make this museum piece for a bacchanalian feast: make all the guests wear togas (a sheet and two safety pins!) and help another museum piece enjoy being twenty-nine (XXIX) again.

This cake is an orgy of chocolate and the muted colours produce a certain authenticity, but you could also make the mosaic pieces from fondant icing, which would give you a wider range of colours, allowing you to reproduce some more modern mosaic designs.

INGREDIENTS

25 cm (10 inch) square chocolate sponge cake (p.9)
100 g (4 oz) chewy chocolate covering made with dark chocolate (p.16)
100 g (4 oz) chewy chocolate covering made with ¹/₂ milk and ¹/₂ white chocolate with red colouring (p.16)
200 g (7 oz) chewy chocolate covering made with white chocolate, a very little milk chocolate and yellow colouring (p.16)
small bar of white chocolate
750 g (1 lb 10 oz) chocolate buttercream (p.17)
300 g (11 oz) coffee buttercream (p.17)
60 g (2¹/₄ oz) chopped roast hazelnuts
small piece of fondant icing (p.15), optional
gold lustre powder

OTHER MATERIALS

35 cm (14 inch) square cake board (drum), covered with black sticky-back plastic

SPECIAL EQUIPMENT

non-stick baking paper
ruler
set square
tracing paper
masking tape
2 flat boards or trays

1 Roll out the three chewy chocolate coverings one colour at a time between sheets of non-stick baking paper, to areas about 3 mm (¹/₈ inch) thick. Cut into 1 cm (¹/₂ inch) squares with a sharp knife, using a ruler and set square for more accuracy.

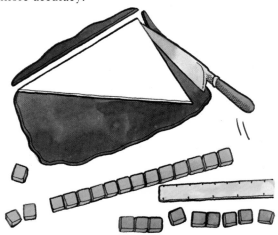

2 Draw your chosen design onto some tracing paper, turn the paper over and tape it down with masking tape onto a flat board or tray (not a table top). Tape down a sheet of non-stick baking paper on top.

3 Starting with the dark chewy chocolate covering, position the 'tiles' around the outline of the design, trimming the pieces to shape with a sharp knife to ensure that they butt together successfully. Following the photograph or your own design, fill in the pattern with the red and yellow colours, cutting squares from the small white chocolate bar for the highlights.

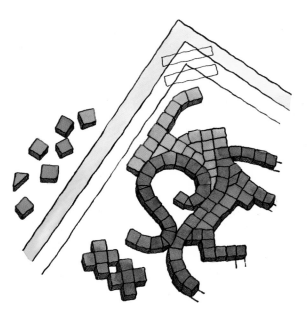

4 Trim the chocolate sponge level, roughly tear off one corner and cut the whole cake in half horizontally. Position one half in the centre of the cake board and spread with a third of the chocolate buttercream, hollowing it a little at the centre to keep the top cake level when you put it on.

5 Spread the other cake half with the coffee buttercream, allowing a little to go down the sides, and carefully place, iced side down, on top of the completed chocolate mosaic design. Cover the bottom of the cake with another flat board or tray and invert the whole thing so that all the chocolate mosaic pieces stick to the coffee buttercream and your design is now the right way round. Remove the board and taped-on paper carefully.

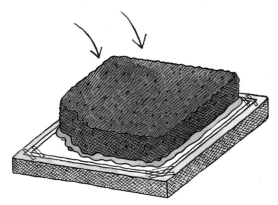

6 Carefully position the mosaic cake on top of the other cake on the black board and cover the sides with the remaining chocolate buttercream. Press the chopped hazelnuts around the sides of the cake to resemble gravel.

7 To make the numeral plate, roll out the spare piece of fondant icing, cut out a small oblong piece and press an inscription into it with a blunt knife. Allow to dry for a short time, position on the board and brush with gold lustre colour mixed with a little water, to give a brass appearance.

ORLANDO

Beware of making this cake for a dedicated cat lover! The mere thought of plunging a knife into an edible effigy of a beloved moggy is enough to give a serious feline fancier the vapours. A lot of cake is used in this creation so you will have to make it for people with healthy appetites for this particular kind of cat food.

Although a rich fruit cake is used, I have made it previously with an orange and white marbled sponge to reflect the colour theme. Light fruit cake with some crystallized ginger or extra orange peel might also be appropriate for a ginger cat, or you could make chocolate sponge for a brown cat.

INGREDIENTS

two 15 cm (6 inch) round rich fruit cakes (p.7)

20 cm (8 inch) square rich fruit cake (p.7)

apricot glaze (p.17)

750 g (1 lb 10 oz) marzipan (p.15)

icing sugar for dusting

1.5 kg (3 lb 6 oz) fondant icing (p.15)

basic paste food colours: orange, yellow, pink, brown, black, blue

OTHER MATERIALS

33 × 20 cm (13 × 8 inch) cake board (drum), cut from a 33 cm (13 inch) square and then covered with silver cake board paper

cocktail stick

length of fine brass, copper or fuse wire, or fishing line

SPECIAL EQUIPMENT

metal skewer or modelling tools

absorbent kitchen paper

fine artist's paint brush

long-bladed knife

small pointed scissors

NOTE: Allow at least 1 day extra preparation time for marzipan to dry.

1 Cut up the cakes as shown in the diagram: cut the square cake in half. Trim short end of one but slice off the end of the other half about two-thirds along – the small piece will be the head. Trim both the round cakes so that they are flat on one side. Trim all the cakes level.

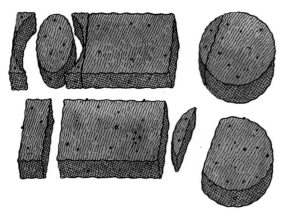

2 Position the larger piece from the square cake on the cake board, and brush one end with apricot glaze. Roll out 50 g (2 oz) of the marzipan to fit this end of the cake. Brush the flat cut side of one of the round cakes with apricot glaze and attach it to the cake on the board, sandwiching the piece of marzipan in between. Brush the top of this keyhole-shape cake with apricot glaze.

3 Roll out 100 g (4 oz) of marzipan to roughly cover the top of the cake and place in position. Now brush the bottom of the smaller straight piece of cake with apricot glaze and place it on top of the larger straight piece. Brush the end of this with glaze, take the remaining round cake and stick it on top of the other round cake in exactly the same way, using a further 50 g (2 oz) of marzipan to join them.

4 Carve the piece of cake for the head into a rough ball. Attach it on top of the straight end of the keyhole-shaped cake using a cocktail stick.

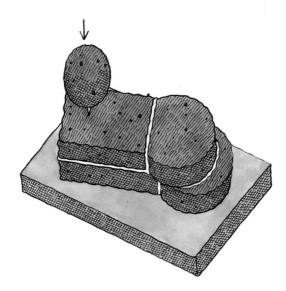

5 Carefully carve the whole cake into the rough shape of a cat, but ignoring details like the face and ears, the paws and the tail. When you are happy with the shape, and remembering that you can add to it later but cannot easily remove cake once the marzipan is on, brush the cake all over with apricot glaze.

6 Roll out the remaining marzipan on an icing sugar dusted surface to an area large enough to completely cover the cake, like a blanket. Lift this gently onto the cake and smooth all over with your hands, easing into the curves. Cut off any excess at the base and use this to patch up any bare areas, smoothing together the joins. Leave the marzipan to dry for at least 24 hours.

7 Reserve 250 g (9 oz) of the fondant for the eyes, nose and mat (keep tightly wrapped in a plastic bag). Colour half of the rest orange, a further quarter a lighter shade of tangerine, and the last quarter cream. Take little bits of all of these colours and use to build up the muzzle shape of the face and to accentuate the cat's backbone and the top curve of the back legs.

8 Use about two-thirds of each fondant colour to cover the cake – keep the rest tightly wrapped in plastic to prevent drying. On an icing sugar dusted surface, lay a long tapering sausage of the orange fondant (about the length of the back of the cat), then smaller orange sausages either side of it, like a fish backbone. Roll sausages of the tangerine fondant and position them around the orange, then do the same with the cream (see diagram). Push all the pieces together and roll lightly together with a rolling pin. You should have something that resembles a thick, ginger, tiger-skin rug. Break up any large areas of orange by cutting a piece out and inserting a piece of another shade pulled from the edge. Keep working the fondant, rolling it thinner with each addition until it is much larger than the cake.

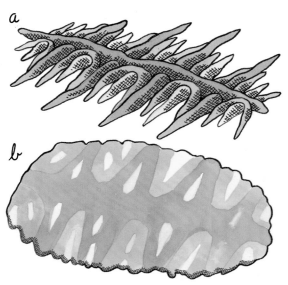

9 Dampen the cake all over with a little water applied with your fingers. Dry your hands and lift the fondant carefully onto the cake, positioning the central line down the middle of the back. Smooth down all over, easing into the cat shape. Cut off the excess from round the base and use pieces of these offcuts to fill in the gaps around the front end of the cat, matching the pattern together and smoothing the joins.

10 With the reserved third of each fondant colour, repeat the process of making stripes as before on an icing sugar dusted surface – but on a much smaller scale this time to fit the face. Roll out and place over the head cake,

smoothing together the joins. Use a skewer or modelling tools to fashion the features on the face – with a sharp pointed knife, cut out and remove the fondant where the eyes go, dampen the area and insert small balls of yellow fondant. Colour a little fondant pink to make the tip of the nose, dampen the area and attach, smoothing into the surrounding fondant.

11 Roll out thinly a smallish piece of striped fondant and then a piece of the lightest cream fondant on an icing sugar dusted surface. Place the cream on top of the other piece and roll together. Cut out two triangles for the ears and shape them round your thumb before applying to the cake with a dampened brush. Tuck small balls of absorbent kitchen paper into the ears to support them while they dry.

12 Use up all the leftover striped fondant to make the front and back legs, paws and tail. Simply roll sausages of fondant and attach to the cake with a little water, modelling the toes with a skewer or a modelling tool.

13 With a fine paint brush and pink food colouring, tint the mouth, the area around the eyes and inside the ears; then with a gingery-brown colour, paint hairs inside the ears, and around the eyebrows and cheeks. Paint a line around the eyes with a very dark brown and paint the pupils black. Cut short lengths of wire or fishing line for whiskers.

14 To make the mat, colour the remaining fondant dark blue. Roll and cut out pieces to cover the cake board, butting them up to the cake and allowing them to overhang at the front and back. Trim the edges and use small pointed scissors to snip in fringing.

bATMOBILE

The streets of Gotham city are strangely silent . . . Holy rolling pins! Someone has swapped the Caped Crusader's classy car for a crazy cake! Who is responsible for this toothsome trick? Why have they left this marzipanned machine? And where are the Dynamic Duo??? This basic method can be used to make any car, if you are not a Batfan, although extra cake will be needed for the top of a saloon car. Toys are available of most models of car and are useful to get the proportions right.

INGREDIENTS

18 cm (7 inch) square rich fruit cake (p.7)

15 cm (6 inch) square rich fruit cake (p.7)

apricot glaze (p.17)

750 g (1 lb 10 oz) marzipan (p.15)

icing sugar for dusting

1.75 kg (3 lb 15 oz) fondant icing (p.15)

basic paste food colours: red, black

225 g (8 oz) royal icing (p.14)

silver lustre powder

OTHER MATERIALS

38 × 18 cm (15 × 7 inch) cake board (drum), cut from a 38 cm (15 inch) square and then covered with red sticky-back plastic

2 cocktail sticks

small sheet of acetate or other clear plastic

SPECIAL EQUIPMENT

medium and fine artist's paint brushes

5 cm (2 inch) round cutter

2.5 cm (1 inch) round cutter

pen top, skewer or tip of a knife

tape measure

ruler

pencil

tracing or greaseproof paper

scissors

paper piping bags

No. 2 writing tube

NOTE: Allow at least 1 day extra preparation time for marzipan to dry.

1 Cut 2.5 cm (1 inch) off one side of the 15 cm (6 inch) square cake and 5 cm (2 inches) off one side of the 18 cm (7 inch) square cake. Brush one short side of each cake with apricot glaze. Roll out 50 g (2 oz) of marzipan on an icing sugar dusted surface to make a rectangle approximately 7.5 × 13 cm (3 × 5 inches). Sandwich the marzipan between the two cakes to make a long slab.

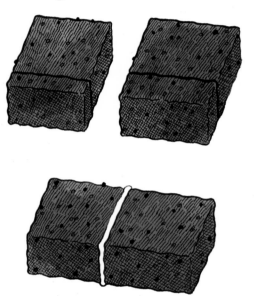

2 Roughly carve the cake into the shape of the car, cutting out the driving compartment (including a raised seat), and sloping the car bonnet. Ignore any fine details such as batfins and doors at this stage. Carve around the top of the wheels to make the wheel arches and round off the cake under the front, back and sides between the wheels. Remember that you can always add to the shape later if you cut away too much, but you cannot easily remove cake once the marzipan is on. Position the cake on the cake board and brush all over with apricot glaze, including under the front, back and sides between the wheels.

3 Roll out 175 g (6 oz) of the marzipan on an icing sugar dusted surface to make a strip long enough to cover one side of the car. Press the marzipan strip onto the side of the cake and tuck under; smooth the marzipan into the wheel arches and trim off any excess. Repeat with a further 175 g (6 oz) of marzipan for the other side of the car.

4 Roll out the remaining marzipan on an icing sugar dusted surface to make a strip approximately 13 × 58 cm (5 × 23 inches), which is long and wide enough to cover the cake from under the front, over the bonnet, into the interior, over the seats, the back, and under the back. Lay the piece over the cake, tucking the ends firmly under with a knife and pressing carefully into the shape of the car. Smooth together the joins and trim off any excess fondant. Use up any offcuts to build up and neaten the insides of the doors and to fill any holes or gaps. Leave to dry for at least 24 hours.

5 Colour 150 g (5½ oz) of the fondant red and wrap well in cling film or a plastic bag. Colour a further 100 g (4 oz) light grey, 250 g (9 oz) dark grey and the rest black. Wrap up separately as before and keep until needed.

6 Roll 4 small sausages of the dark grey fondant, flatten and press underneath the wheel arches. Roll out strips of the rest of the dark grey fondant to cover the underside of the sides, front and back. Dampen these areas with a dampened brush and press the fondant pieces into position, tucking them under and neatening with a knife.

7 Use sausages of black fondant attached with a dampened brush to build up the front bumper of the car, the ridge down the centre of the bonnet, either side of the bonnet where the headlights are, the ridge around the front and back windscreens, the top of the doors and the fins along the back. Make two long sausages for the ridges along each side of the car: these extend from the front of the car, over each wheel arch and along the side. Smooth all these pieces into the marzipan.

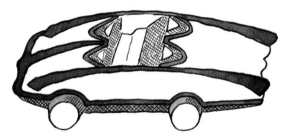

8 Roll out 100 g (4 oz) of the black fondant on an icing sugar dusted surface and cut two long strips to fit each side of the cake between the wheels and below the ridge. Dampen these areas with a little water on a brush and attach the strips to the car.

9 Roll out a further 200 g (7 oz) of black fondant and, using the 5 cm (2 inch) cutter or a plastic tub, cut out four circles for the wheels. Attach onto the car with a little water. Roll out 75 g (3 oz) of the light grey fondant and cut out four circles with the smaller 2.5 cm (1 inch) cutter. With this same cutter, cut into the centre of the black wheels and pull away the fondant. Press the light grey circles into these holes and impress some detail into them with a pen top, skewer or tip of a knife.

10 Reserving a small piece for extra details, roll out the red fondant to fit the seating area. Dampen this area on the cake with a little water and tuck the red fondant into place, easing over the seat and smoothing down well.

11 Roll out the remaining black fondant to make a strip long enough to cover the cake from front to back, similar to the marzipan strip in step 4 but starting at the front bumper level, extending over the bonnet, straight across the seat area, over the back to the back bumper level (it needs to be approximately 38 cm/15 inches long and wide enough to cover the cake from side ridge to side ridge, approximately 19 cm/7½ inches). These lengths can be measured on the cake with a tape measure for accuracy. Cut the sides of the strip straight against a ruler, dampen the marzipan in these areas with a little water on a brush and apply the strip of fondant, smoothing down well. Trim off any excess round the wheel and at the front and back with a sharp knife.

12 Carefully slit the black fondant now covering the red seat area, pull it away and fold it down inside the edges of the car. Use up some of the fondant offcuts to cover any bare areas that show inside the car.

13 Use up any black fondant offcuts to build up the steering column and, with a little of the remaining red, the piece between the seats. Make three thin tapering sausages of the remaining black fondant, fold in the middle and press onto the back of the car to make the chevrons.

14 Break the cocktail sticks in half and dampen them with a little water. Roll the remaining red fondant into three thin sausages, insert a cocktail stick in each and roll again until smooth. Cut a little of the fondant away to expose the points of the sticks and push them into the back of the cake.

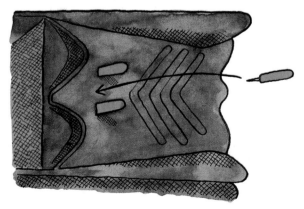

15 Roll out the remaining light grey fondant fairly thinly on an icing sugar dusted surface and cut out pieces to make the head and tail lights and grilles. Attach these with a little water applied with a brush.

16 Trace in pencil the template shown here onto tracing or greaseproof paper, cut out and use as a guide to cut four windscreens from the clear acetate. Push these into position on the cake and cut out a small strip of acetate to fit between them. Push into place. Cut a small circle of acetate for the steering wheel.

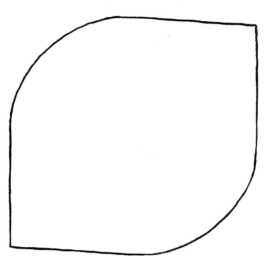

17 Colour half the royal icing red and half grey. Place the grey icing in a paper piping bag with a No. 2 writing tube and pipe the steering wheel onto the circle of acetate. Pipe the same colour round the edges of the windscreen.

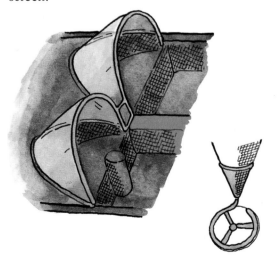

18 Place the red icing in another paper bag with a No. 2 writing tube and pipe along the sides, the fins and round the headlights, back lights and grilles. Pipe a bat logo on the driver's door. Attach the now fairly dry steering wheel to the column with a blob of grey icing.

19 With a fine artist's paint brush, mix the silver lustre powder with a little water and paint all the light grey areas of fondant and royal icing to give a silver effect.

Canned Fruit

A friend at art school used to keep her coloured pencils in a printed can that once contained walnuts. I made a life-size cake replica of this for her twenty-first birthday, one of the first fantasy cakes I ever made.

A faithful reproduction of a food can or package makes an impressive and personal cake, especially if it is a favourite food or the trademark is a relevant name. This was Andy Warhol's favourite brand of soup or, at least, the one he chose to paint in the 1960s when the Pop Art movement was at its height.

Enlarge your chosen can label to the required size for this larger-than-life cake on a photocopier, and copy it as accurately as possible on the cake for maximum impact.

INGREDIENTS

quantity for 15 cm (6 inch) round, rich fruit cake (p.7), divided between two 882 g (1 lb 15 oz) cans

apricot glaze (p.17)

400 g (14 oz) marzipan (p.15)

icing sugar for dusting

550 g (1 lb 3 oz) fondant icing (p.15)

basic paste food colours: red, yellow, black

opaque white food colour

OTHER MATERIALS

15 cm (6 inch) square cake board (drum), covered with black sticky-back plastic

SPECIAL EQUIPMENT

piece of string

non-stick baking paper

small round cutter or lid

tracing paper

soft pencil

fine artist's paint brushes

NOTE: Allow at least 1 day extra preparation time for marzipan to dry.

1 Plan your can design on paper, tracing off a real can as necessary but taking into account that the thickness of the marzipan and icing will add to the finished dimensions of the cake.

2 Cut the tops of the cakes so that they are level; they should be approximately 7.5 cm (3 inches) deep. Brush the tops with apricot glaze. Roll out 50 g (2 oz) of the marzipan on an icing sugar dusted surface to make an 11 cm (4½ inch) diameter circle. Sandwich this between the cakes (first brushed with glaze) and if necessary use small pieces of marzipan to neaten the join.

3 Measure round the cake with a piece of string to work out the circumference (approximately 34 cm/13½ inches) and the total depth of the cake (approximately 16 cm/6½ inches). On an icing sugar dusted surface, roll out 300 g (11 oz) of the marzipan and trim to an oblong of these dimensions. Brush the sides of the cake with some more apricot glaze, lay the cake sideways on the marzipan strip and roll it up, to cover with the marzipan. Brush the top of the cake with apricot glaze. Gather up the offcuts and add to the remaining marzipan. Form the marzipan into a ball, and roll flat into a circle to fit the top of the cake. Position on, trim round and work the marzipan joins together with the flat blade of a knife. Leave to dry on a sheet of non-stick baking paper for 24 hours.

4 Colour 200 g (7 oz) of the fondant red and 15 g (½ oz) golden yellow, and keep tightly wrapped until needed. On an icing sugar dusted surface, roll out 200 g (7 oz) of the white fondant and cut out a rectangle approximately 8.5 cm (3¼ inches) by 35 cm (14 inches). Dampen the marzipan cake all over with a little water and as with the marzipan, roll just the bottom half of the cake up in the white fondant.

5 Roll out the red fondant to the same dimensions as the white rectangle and wrap round the top half of the cake in the same way, smoothing together the joins at the back. Position the cake in the centre of the cake board.

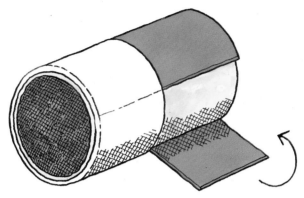

6 With a small round cutter or spice jar lid, cut a central circle out of the front of the red and white icing where they join and prise the fondant away from the cake. Roll the yellow icing into a ball, roll out slightly and cut out with the same cutter. Insert the yellow circle into the hole on the cake and smooth together the joins.

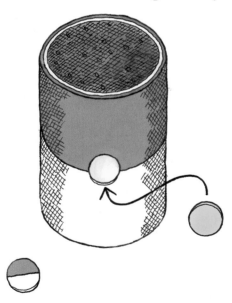

7 Trace the main heading for the can onto tracing paper and then go over the back with a soft pencil. Place the paper the right way up over the red icing and trace over the lettering again – a soft line will transfer to the icing. Then, with a sharp knife, cut and prise out the

red fondant where the white lettering will go. Use 20 g (¾ oz) of white fondant to fill in the letters, pressing small pieces into the holes in the red fondant. Smooth the surfaces together with your fingers.

8 Trace the small white lettering onto tracing paper, turn over and this time paint over the back of the lines with white food colouring using a fine artist's paint brush. Place the paper the right way up over the icing and gently retrace onto the cake as before with a pencil – the wording will come off in white on the icing. Remove the paper and paint over with more white food colouring to strengthen the lines and make it clearer to read.

9 Trace all the other lettering onto tracing paper, then turn over, retrace and transfer to the cake with a pencil as before in step 7. Fill in

as necessary with red and black paste food colours thinned with a little water, applying with a fine paint brush. With black, paint the shadows on the main lettering and the design on the yellow disc. With thinned yellow paste food colour, paint the repeat fleur-de-lys design near the bottom of the cake on the white icing.

10 Colour the remaining fondant light grey. On an icing sugar dusted surface, roll 75 g (3 oz) of it into a ball and roll into a circle to fit the top of the cake. Attach to the cake with a little water and then lightly press various glasses, cups or jars into it to make the ridges of the tin. Roll the remaining grey fondant into two sausages to form rims round the top and bottom edge of the cake. Attach with a little water and work together the joins at the back with your fingers.

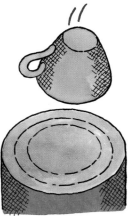

11 Finally, with a brush and black food colouring, paint shadows around the ridges in the top of the tin, and around the sides of the rims at the top and bottom of the cake.

CURRANTCY

The Duchess of Windsor is supposed to have said that one can never be too rich or too thin. If you have no hope of being either, this wedge of fruit cake forgery is some consolation – it is about as close as most of us will get to anything rich although it won't even help with the slimming diet.

Copy a real banknote to the best of your ability (but don't make a career out of it!) and change the denomination for a 21st or any other anniversary celebration. You could even add a further message on the bands.

INGREDIENTS
18 cm (7 inch) square rich fruit cake (p.17)
apricot glaze (p.17)
450 g (1 lb) marzipan (p.15)
icing sugar for dusting
500 g (1 lb 2 oz) fondant icing (p.15)
basic paste food colours: violet, orange, green, blue, black, pink

OTHER MATERIALS
20 cm (8 inch) square cake board (drum), covered with gold cake board paper

SPECIAL EQUIPMENT
ruler
small glass bottle, tumbler or icing smoothers
soft pencil
tracing or greaseproof paper
£20 banknote
fine artist's paint brush
white plate
sheet of white paper
absorbent kitchen paper

NOTE: Allow at least 1½ days extra preparation time for marzipan and fondant to dry.

1 If necessary, trim the cake to level it, turn it over so that you will be decorating the smooth bottom of the cake and cut out as shown in the diagram: trim a 1.5 cm (¾ inch) strip off opposite sides of the cake, but cutting only just over half way to create a staggered double-rectangle shape. Cut against a ruler to achieve straight lines. Position the cake on the cake board and brush with apricot glaze.

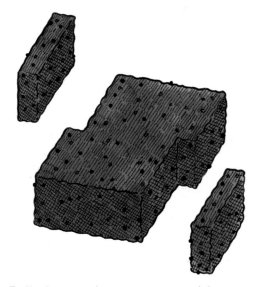

2 Roll the marzipan out on an icing sugar dusted surface and cover the cake in the same basic way as you would a square cake (p.22), cutting eight pieces to fit round all the sides then covering the top with two rectangular pieces, one for each pile of notes. Smooth together the joins and flatten the cake all over with a small glass bottle, tumbler or icing smoothers, trying to get the corners as neat and square as possible. Leave to dry for at least 24 hours.

3 Dampen the sides of the cake with a little water on your fingers. Using 450 g (1 lb) of the fondant icing, cover the entire cake in sections in the same way as you did the marzipan, rolling it out on an icing sugar dusted surface. Smooth together the joins and flatten all over as before.

4 Press the back of a knife horizontally into the fondant all the way round the sides of the cake to make it look like a stack of notes. Leave to dry for 12 hours or overnight.

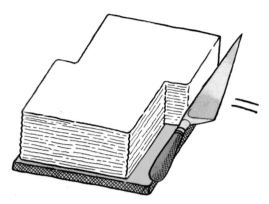

5 With a pencil and tracing or greaseproof paper, trace the basic outlines of the design off a real £20 banknote, ignoring the central 2.5 cm (1 inch) as it will be covered by the paper strap, and altering the denomination to your chosen figure (I used 21). Turn the paper over, go over the back of the design with a soft pencil, turn back again and trace onto the top of the icing. You may need to go over the back of the paper again to successfully trace the design down a second time.

6 With a fine paint brush, paint in the banknote design on the top of the cake, trying as far as possible not to lean your hand on the cake

(resting your arm on a pile of books helps). Use a white plate for a palette to mix the colours (violet, orange, green, blue, black and pink) and test them on a sheet of white paper before applying to the cake (see p.23 for painting tips). Start with the light-coloured areas first, mixing the paste colour with water, and work towards the darker details, finishing with the dark purple lettering and the black numbers (date of birth if this is a birthday cake!). Try not to use the brush too wet or the colours will run; absorbent kitchen paper makes a good blotter. Work on both notes in stages at the same time otherwise you might finish one and be unable to copy it again in exactly the same way.

7 Colour the remaining fondant pale green to make the retaining strip (a little black added will give a nice dingy colour). Roll it into a sausage approximately 18 cm (7 inches) long on an icing sugar dusted surface, then flatten it with a rolling pin to make a strip 9 cm (3½ inches) wide. Slice this into two long strips 4 cm (1½ inches) wide, using a ruler to obtain a straight edge. Dampen the centre of the top and long sides of the cake with a little water on a brush and wrap the green strips over, pressing into position, smoothing flat and trimming neatly around the base. Press the back of a knife into the sides of these strips at four horizontal intervals to make them look like separate wads of money.

WHITE CHRISTMAS

I remember once trying to eat a plaster snowman off a Christmas cake, convinced, with a child's logic, that if it was on a cake it must be edible. Well, all the decorations (except of course the candle) on this and all the other cakes in this book are edible; in fact in making these trees I have at last found a good use for angelica, having previously only ever seen it cut into little diamonds. The glass-like background is quite straightforward to make from clear mint boiled sweets and blue powder food colouring.

INGREDIENTS

20 cm (8 inch) round rich fruit cake (p.7)
apricot glaze (p.17)
650 g (1 lb 7 oz) marzipan (p.15)
icing sugar for dusting
butter or margarine for greasing
2 yellow boiled sweets
200 g (7 oz) clear mint boiled sweets
blue food colour powder
750 g (1 lb 10 oz) fondant icing (p.15)
150 g (5½ oz) whole angelica
225 g (8 oz) royal icing (p.14)
basic paste food colours: brown, black, green, red

OTHER MATERIALS

25 cm (10 inch) round cake board (drum)
small blue candle or taper candle

SPECIAL EQUIPMENT

small five-pointed star cutter
non-stick baking paper
metal baking tray
20 cm (8 inch) round loose-bottomed cake tin
medium and fine artist's paint brushes
pair of pliers
2 paper piping bags (p.19)
holly leaf cutter

NOTE: Allow at least 1 day extra preparation time for marzipan to dry.

1 Position the fruit cake the right way up on the cake board. Roughly carve the front edges of the cake to give a more rounded shape (the natural risen shape of the cake will help this). Brush the sides of the cake with apricot glaze. Roll out 150 g (5½ oz) of the marzipan on an icing sugar dusted surface into a sausage approximately 40 cm (16 inches) long, tapering at the ends. Position it round the bottom of the front of the cake, to accentuate the hill shape.

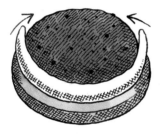

2 Brush the whole cake with more apricot glaze. On an icing sugar dusted surface, roll out the remaining marzipan to a circle large enough to cover the whole cake. Lift this marzipan circle onto the cake and smooth down all round with your hands, trimming and neatening at the base as necessary. Leave to dry for at least 24 hours.

3 Grease the inside of the five-pointed star cutter and line it with a strip of non-stick baking paper. Place a sheet of non-stick baking paper on a metal baking tray and put the lined star shape on this. Chop the yellow boiled sweets and fill the star cutter.

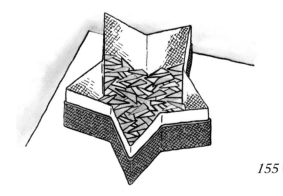

4 Cook at 190°C (375°F/Gas Mark 5) for 4–5 minutes until completely melted. Take out and leave to cool for 15 minutes, when the sweet should be hard and cool enough to carefully push out of the cutter mould. Gently peel off any paper stuck to the sugar star.

5 Grease and line the 20 cm (8 inch) round loose-bottomed cake tin with a single thickness of non-stick baking paper (p.20). Grease and paper the *outside* of the star cutter and place it in the lined cake tin. Chop up the clear mints into fragments as before. With a dry brush, dust the base of the lined tin around the star cutter with blue powder colour and cover with the chopped mints in an even layer. Place in the hot oven 190°C (375°F/Gas Mark 5) for 5 minutes or until completely melted. Remove and leave to cool for 5 minutes. With pliers, as it will still be too hot to touch, start to pull the star cutter out. If the sugar is still not set, cool a little longer.

6 Pull out any paper that should have come out with the star cutter and place the yellow sugar star in the hole. Put the whole thing back into the hot oven for just 1 minute so that the star and blue sky fuse together. Take out and leave to cool completely before gently easing the blue sky background out of the tin. Pull away any paper that may have stuck, lay the circle on a flat surface and with a sharp knife carefully pare off any excess sugar around the side where the hot sugar will have bubbled up the side of the tin.

7 On an icing sugar dusted surface, roll out 600 g (1 lb 5 oz) of the fondant icing to a circle approximately 35 cm (14 inches) in diameter. Lift this icing over the cake and smooth down all round, trimming at the bottom to neaten. Reserve the trimmings for the holly.

8 Colour the remaining fondant icing reddish-brown and shape into a simple small house with a chimney. Position on the cake with a little water, and paint on windows and a door with a fine artist's brush and dark brown or black food colouring.

9 With a sharp knife, cut the angelica into small flat sheets and cut out the tree shapes (see diagrams). Slot the pieces into each other to assemble the trees and press into the white fondant on the cake, remembering to avoid the back of the cake where the sky will go.

10 Fill a paper piping bag with half the royal icing. Snip a small hole in the end and pipe snow along the tops of the boughs of the trees, small lines on the house for window sills and along the top of the door, and around the edge of the roof. Cut the hole in the icing bag a little bigger and pipe in the whole of the roof, pushing the icing around with the tip of a wet knife to give a smooth finish.

11 Colour two-thirds of the reserved fondant trimmings green and the rest red. Roll out the green fondant on an icing sugar dusted board and cut out holly leaf shapes with a cutter. Roll tiny balls of the red fondant. Place the remaining royal icing in the second paper piping bag, snip a small hole in the end and pipe small dots around the bottom of the cake to secure the leaves and berries, attaching them as you go.

12 Cut a slot in the cake towards the back to fit the sugar sky in. Use the loose bottom of the cake tin to check the fit, prising out any excess cake to accommodate it. Carefully push the sugar sky piece into the slot.

13 Finally, push a taper candle into the cake approximately 1.5 cm (¾ inch) behind the star. Light this when you present the cake, to make the star shine. Do not leave the lighted candle unattended however; the candle will burn down quickly and could ruin the cake.

*f*IRST PRIZE VEG

I wasn't at all green fingered until I made this cake – the green colouring got under my nails and took some scrubbing to remove! Prize-winning gardeners will appreciate this tribute to their ability, a pleasant change from the usual floral designs. Extend the idea to making other giant vegetables and you may even fool the judges at the county show.

Flavouring is a bit of a problem as marrow itself is rather lacking in taste. Vanilla seems acceptable to me but you may like to shock with something stronger like lemon or, more in keeping with the green colour, mint buttercream.

INGREDIENTS

23 cm (9 inch) square sponge cake (p.9)

20 cm (8 inch) square sponge cake (p.9)

750 g (1 lb 10 oz) fondant icing (p.15)

basic paste food colours: red, yellow, green, black or brown

icing sugar for dusting

600 g (1 lb 5 oz) buttercream (p.17)

liquid food colour: green

apricot glaze (p.17)

gold lustre powder

OTHER MATERIALS

30 × 15 cm (12 × 6 inch) cake board, cut from a 30 cm (12 inch) square and then covered with red gingham sticky-back plastic

wooden skewer

SPECIAL EQUIPMENT

4 cm (1½ inch) round cutter

non-stick baking paper

paper piping bags

fine artist's paint brush

1 First make the prize rosette: colour 75 g (3 oz) of the fondant red. On an icing sugar dusted surface, roll out approximately 15 g (½ oz) of the white fondant icing and cut out a small circle using the 4 cm (1½ inch) round cutter. Place this on a piece of non-stick baking paper. Roll out the red fondant fairly thinly, cut out the two pointed bottom ribbons and press these onto the white circle towards the bottom edge. Cut a strip of red fondant approximately 1.5 cm (¾ inch) wide. Attach around the white circle, pleating and pressing on as you go. A little water will help it stick. Roll out a further 15 g (½ oz) of white fondant, cut out a 4 cm (1½ inch) circle as before and attach this on top of the other circle with a little water to cover the edges of the red fondant. Leave to dry while preparing the rest of the cake.

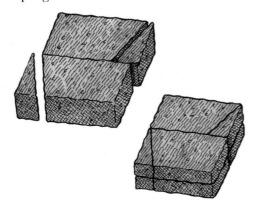

2 Cut up both cakes as shown in the diagrams: cut each in half vertically and then trim off the opposite outside ends of each half diagonally. Cut the pieces from the 20 cm (8 inch) cake in half again horizontally to create the four layers of sponge.

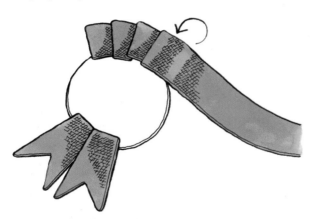

3 On a wooden board, assemble all the pieces as shown, with the larger cakes sandwiched between the thinner ones. Then, with a sharp knife, carve the whole construction into the shape of a marrow, remembering to carve under and around the ends to achieve the necessary rounded shape.

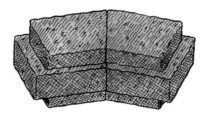

4 Colour the buttercream pale green with liquid food colour. Reassemble the cake pieces on the gingham-covered cake board, sandwiching them together and filling any bad holes, cracks or uneven areas with half the buttercream. Brush all over with apricot glaze.

5 With paste colours, colour 15 g (½ oz) of the fondant icing cream and 75 g (3 oz) pale green and reserve, tightly wrapped. Colour the remaining fondant a deep green and divide it into five pieces. On an icing sugar dusted surface, roll each piece, one at a time, into a long sausage, flatten it with a rolling pin and cut into an elongated oval that is thicker in the middle and pointed at both ends, and is the length of the cake marrow.

6 Place the oval pieces one at a time on the cake, 1 cm (½ inch) apart, and use up the offcuts to make small triangle-shaped pieces to go under the ends to suggest the green stripes underneath the marrow.

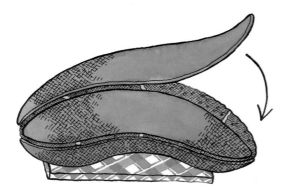

7 Roll the 15 g (½ oz) piece of cream fondant into a ball, flatten it with a rolling pin and cut round the edge with a sharp knife to make a rough star shape. Stick this onto the thick end of the marrow with a little water to hide the area where the points of the green fondant come together.

8 Roll the 75 g (3 oz) piece of pale-green fondant into a slightly tapering sausage 10 cm (4 inches) long. Press a wooden skewer into this all round to give a ridged effect and twist it a little. Trim one end flat and pull the other end out a bit into a star shape to look like the base of the stalk. Dampen the wooden skewer with a little water and push it into the centre of the base end, through the centre of the pale-green stalk. The stalk is now on a firm skewer base which can be pushed securely into the narrow end of the marrow cake.

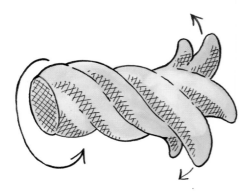

9 Use two-thirds of the remaining buttercream to fill the gaps between the green fondant sections: place the buttercream into a paper piping bag, snip a fairly large hole in the end and pipe a thick line along each gap before spreading around to fill with the point of a knife. Use several bags to do this, taking care not to overfill them as the buttercream quickly warms up and becomes too soft to handle.

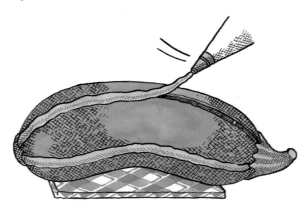

10 Place the remaining buttercream in another paper piping bag, snip a small hole in the end and pipe small dots and lines all over the dark green fondant icing to give some texture to the marrow.

11 With a fine brush, paint a message or numeral on the centre of the rosette in either black or light brown food colouring, followed by gold lustre powder mixed with a little water to give a gold finish. Remove the rosette from the non-stick baking paper and position it on the cake board in front of the marrow.

SWISS ROLLER

Most people have an amusing DIY anecdote to tell – mine is stepping on the edge of a roller tray full of ice cream pink paint (not unlike the colour in this cake), and launching the entire contents over myself in true slapstick fashion. Every move I made in an attempt to remove the stuff resulted in spreading it still further until it was all over me, in my hair, on every rag, floor, door handle and tap – in fact it's still on the overalls!

A new home usually means decorating so make this cake for a housewarming party, in the new colour scheme if you can.

INGREDIENTS

two 15 cm (6 inch) round sponge cakes (p.9)
1 Swiss roll cake (p.14)
1 kg (2 lb 4 oz) fondant icing (p.15)
basic paste food colours: pink, black, brown, and other colours of choice
300 g (11 oz) buttercream (p.17)
apricot glaze (p.17)
icing sugar for dusting
175 g (6 oz) glacé icing (p.16)
liquid food colour: pink
silver lustre powder

OTHER MATERIALS

35 cm (14 inch) square cake board, covered in newspaper and then clear sticky-back plastic
small piece (2.5 × 20 cm/1 × 8 inches) of thick card
cling film
cocktail stick

SPECIAL EQUIPMENT

sharp craft knife
ruler
skewer or knitting needle
medium artist's paint brush

1 Colour the fondant icing with paste food colours in the following quantities: 150 g (5½ oz) pink, 250 g (9 oz) grey, 175 g (6 oz) brown, 50 g (2 oz) dark brown, leaving the rest white. Keep all the colours tightly wrapped until needed.

2 Trim the tops of both the round cakes to level and sandwich them together with a third of the buttercream. Position on the cake board and brush all over with apricot glaze. Position the Swiss roll on the board alongside the large cake and cover with the remaining buttercream, roughing up the surface with a fork to resemble a paint roller.

3 With a sharp craft knife, cut the piece of thick card to a rough paint brush shape and cover it with cling film. Take 100 g (4 oz) of the brown fondant, divide it in half and shape into two paint brush handles. Position one on the board near the roller and press the other onto the cardboard shape to cover it completely (keep on one side until later). Cut a hole in end of both handles.

4 Take 50 g (2 oz) of the grey fondant and make two small oblong pieces for the metal bits (ferrule) of the brushes. Position one on the cake board and the other on the cardboard, both pressed against the brown handles. Take the 50 g (2 oz) dark brown fondant and shape into two rough oblongs for the brush bristles. Press these into position and score with a knife.

5 On an icing sugar dusted surface, roll 150 g (5½ oz) of the white fondant to make a strip 5 cm (2 inches) wide and 48 cm (19 inches) long. Cut one long edge straight with a knife against a ruler. Attach this strip, straight edge uppermost, around the bottom of the round cake. Roll out all the pink fondant to a similarly shaped strip, cut both edges straight and position around the middle of the cake, butting up carefully to the white strip. Roll out a further 150 g (5½ oz) of the white fondant, cut both edges straight and position around the cake above the pink strip; it should come just above the height of the cake. Work together the joins at the back of the cake with the flat blade of a knife.

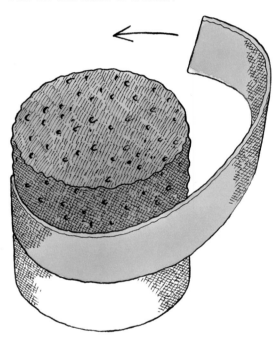

6 Roll out the remaining brown fondant into a fat sausage and press a skewer or knitting needle lengthways all round it to make grooves. Position on the board for the roller handle.

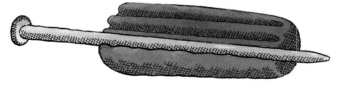

7 Take 25 g (1 oz) of the grey fondant, roll a pea-sized ball from it, then flatten and press a line across it with a knife to look like a screw. Roll the

remainder into two equal-sized balls, flatten and press them onto the ends of the roller cake. Press the screw piece into the centre of one end.

8 Take 25 g (1 oz) of the grey fondant and, on an icing sugar dusted surface, roll out a sausage approximately 20 cm (8 inches) long. This will be the metal part of the roller handle. Break a cocktail stick in half and press one piece, broken end first, into each end of the sausage of grey icing, leaving the points sticking out. Using the cocktail sticks, press one end of the grey sausage into the roller handle, shape the rest in a curve over the paintbrush on the cake board for support, and press the other end into the screw-less end of the roller cake.

9 Take 100 g (4 oz) of the remaining grey fondant and divide into three. On an icing sugar dusted surface, roll one piece into a sausage approximately 48 cm (19 inches) long, flatten to a strip with a rolling pin and wrap inside the white fondant at the top of the paint tin cake. Roll two more similar length sausages from the other two pieces of grey fondant and wrap them around the top and bottom of the paint tin cake, sticking them on with a little water if necessary. Neaten the joined ends.

10 Take the remaining grey fondant and roll into a sausage approximately 30 cm (12 inches) long. Cut off two lengths each 3 cm (1¼ inches) long; lightly fold both in half to make two loops and attach one to each side of the top of the paint tin cake with a little water. Thread one end of the long sausage through each loop and attach to the side of the cake tin with a little water in a long loop, to resemble a handle.

11 Mix up the glacé icing, adding a few drops of pink liquid food colouring. Pour some of the icing into the top of the paint tin and position the paint brush on the cardboard base on top. Pour more icing onto the brush, down the sides of the paint tin cake (a good way to hide messy joins!) and around the cake board in blobs and splashes.

12 Mix silver lustre powder with a little water and, with a medium-size brush, paint all the grey fondant for a metallic effect.

13 With the remaining white fondant, make small paint colour charts: add different amounts of various shades and colours to small pieces of fondant, roll them out on an icing sugar dusted surface, cut roughly to size, butt the different colours together, roll together lightly then trim to size and surround with frames of white fondant.

LIST OF SUPPLIERS

Although the recipes for making icing and marzipan used in this book are quite simple and quick, you may prefer to buy these ingredients ready-made or ready-to-mix, to save time and effort. There are many good quality products on the market, available from most branches of superior supermarkets, grocers and specialist kitchen and baking stores. A few are listed below, and also a list of mail order suppliers for all the products you may need – equipment, icings, marzipan, and food colourings.

Fondant icing can be obtained ready-made from many supermarkets, for instance, to name just three brands, Sainsbury's, Whitworths and Renshaws market 225g (8oz) packets. Many mail-order and retail specialists (see below) make their own icing too. Royal icing is now sold in 500g packets from Whitworths and Silver Spoon among others, and just needs the addition of water. There are many brands of marzipan available – choose a softer, flexible variety if possible. One thing to remember is that, generally, bought icings do take a little longer to dry hard than home-made.

RETAIL OUTLETS

The Cake Hole
525 Upper Elmers
End Road,
Beckenham,
Kent, BR3 3DE
Tel: 01-658-6692
(eve: 01-654-1079)

Cellar Crafts
20 Hookstone Road,
Harrogate,
North Yorks, HG2 8BX
Tel: 0423-871277

Kitchens
167 Whiteladies Road,
Bristol,
Avon, BS8 2SQ
Tel: 0272-739614
and 4–5 Quiet Street,
Bath, Avon, BA1 2JS
Tel: 0225-330524

Quality Cakes
1 Grassmere Parade,
Felpham Village,
Bognor Regis,
West Sussex, PO22 7NT
Tel: 0243-820246

*Speciality Sugarcraft
Products*
143 Quebec Road,
Blackburn,
Lancs, BB2 7DP
Tel: 0254-65762

RETAIL AND
MAIL-ORDER

The Cake Studio
89 High Street,
Lincoln, LN5 7QW
Tel: 0522-23781

*Covent Garden
Kitchen Supplies*
3 North Row,
The Market,
Covent Garden,
London, WC2 8RA
Tel: 01-836-9167

Creating Cakes
The Mall,
123 East Street,
Sittingbourne
Kent, ME10 4BL
Tel: 0795-26358

David Mellor
4 Sloane Square,
London, SW1W 8EE
Tel: 01-730-4259
and 26 James Street,
Covent Garden,
London, WC2E 8PA
Tel: 01-379-6947
and 66 King Street,
Manchester, M2 4NP
Tel: 061-834-7023

Elizabeth Ashley
26 Market Street,
Southport,
Merseyside, PR8 1HJ
Tel: 0704-33095

Elizabeth David Ltd
46 Bourne Street,
London, SW1W 8JD
Tel: 01-730-3123

Homebakers Supplies
157–159 High Street,
Wolstanton,
Newcastle,
Staffs, ST5 0EJ
Tel: 0782-614119

*Jenny Campbell/B. R.
Mathews & Son*
12 Gypsy Hill,
Upper Norwood,
London, SE19 1NN
Tel: 01-670-0788

Lincoln House
Cake Decorating Centre,
198 Desborough Road,
High Wycombe,
Bucks, HP11 2QA
Tel: 0494-30625

*Mary Ford Cake Artistry
Centre Ltd*
28–30 Southbourne Grove,
Southbourne,
Bournemouth,
Dorset, BH6 3RA
Tel: 0202-431001/422653

Midlands Icing Centre
10 Moat Lane,
Great Wyrley,
Nr Walsall,
West Midlands, WS6 6DU
Tel: 0922-410040
and 19 Meadvale Road,
Knighton,
Leicester, LE2 3WN
Tel: 0533-709268

Phoenix Kitchen
349 Ballards Lane,
Tally Ho Corner,
Finchley,
London, N12 8LJ
Tel: 01-445-2921

A Piece of Cake
18 Upper High Street
Thames, Oxon, OX9 3EX
Tel: 084421-3428

Squires Kitchen
The Potteries,
Pottery Lane,
Wrecclesham, Farnham,
Surrey, GU10 4QJ
Tel: 0252-711749

Woodnutt's Ltd
97 Church Road,
Hove,
Sussex, BN3 2BA
Tel: 0273-205353

Ye Olde Cake Shop
88 Coggeshall Road,
Braintree,
Essex, CM7 6BY
Tel: 0376-48678

MAIL-ORDER

Cookcraft Club Ltd
20 Canterbury Road,
Herne Bay,
Kent, CT6 5DJ

Craft Centres
360 Leach Place,
Bamber Bridge,
Preston,
Lancashire, PR5 8AR
Tel: 0772-34848

Guy Paul & Co. Ltd
Unit 84, A1 Industrial Park,
Little End Road,
Eaton Socon,
Cambridgeshire, PE19 3JH
Tel: 0480-72545

Top Tier Sugarcraft
10 Meadow Road,
Balloch,
Inverness-shire, IV1 2JR
Tel: 0463-790456

*i*NDEX

ACKNOWLEDGEMENTS
Thanks to Bobbie, Joanna, Jerry, Mark, Marie, Sally, Edwin, Barbara Frost, Steve Berry, David Read, Realm, Shelley Shoes for the loan of brothel creepers, Judith Downey, Saucerman, and Gibby's Peg. Not forgetting Geoffrey.
The publishers would also like to thank: Alex Corrin for indexing, Mary Lambert for text editing and Janice Murfitt for recipe testing.